GUNNERS AT WAR

1939-1945

GUNNERS AT WAR

1939-1945

PETER MEAD

LONDON

IAN ALLAN LTD

First published 1982

ISBN 0 7110 1157 5

Design by Robert C. Wilcockson

© Peter Mead 1982

Published by Ian Allan Ltd, Shepperton, Surrey;
and printed by Ian Allan Printing Ltd at their works
at Coombelands in Runnymede, England

1
Bofors of 26 LAA Regiment in
the ruins of San Angelo, south
of Cassino. *IWM*

2
Artillery preparation for the
Rhine crossing. *IWM*

Contents

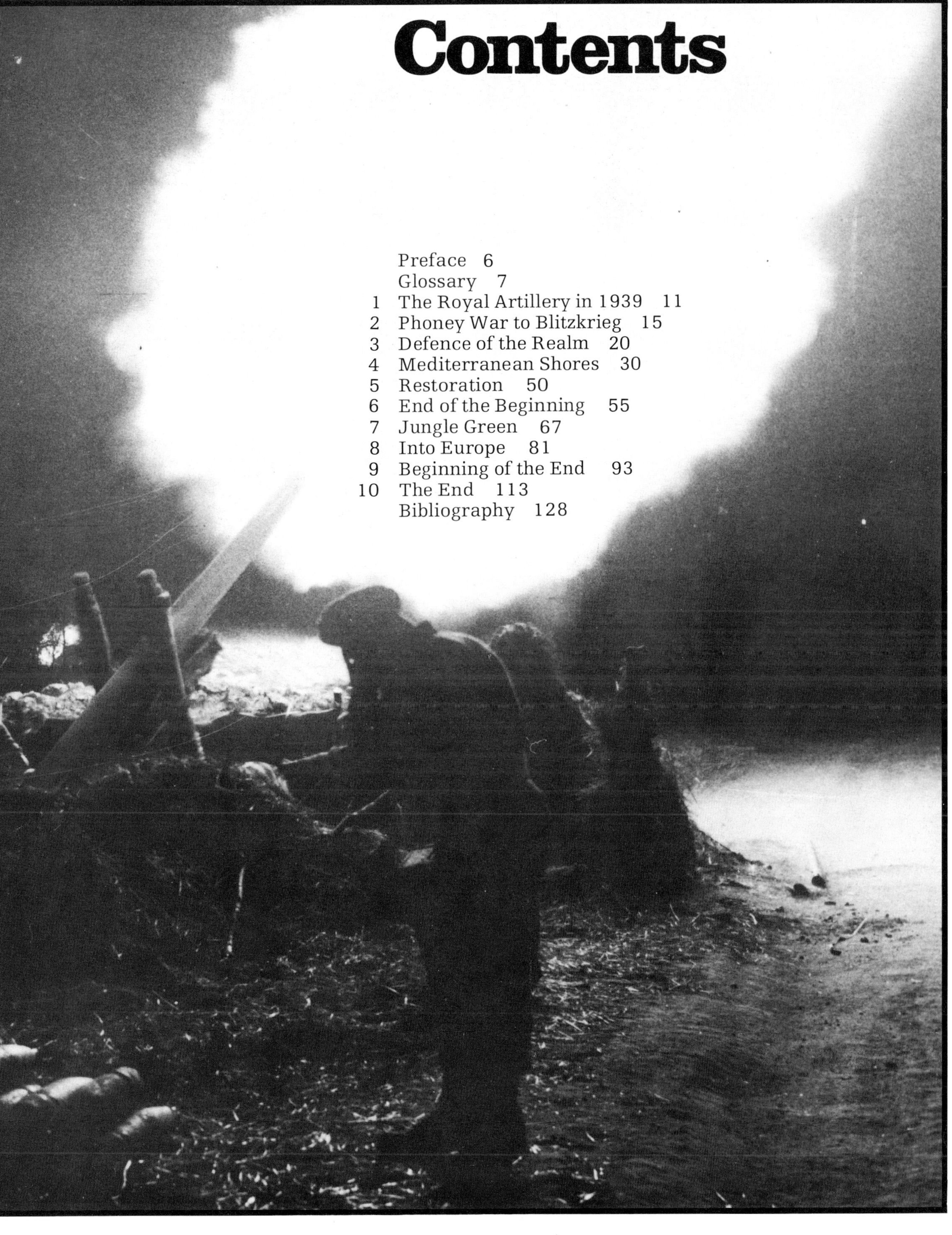

Preface

That no World War 2 series would be complete without a volume on the Gunners, few World War 2 soldiers would dispute. In numbers, and militarily, the artillery was all-pervasive. It was not, however, until I began — within the discipline of the space available — to record something of the Gunners' story that I understood the scale of my task.

It is hardly necessary, perhaps, to warn the reader that this book cannot in any respect constitute a history. In this brief selection of artillery actions and activities in some of the phases of a war of six years in many theatres, much of the Gunner picture is necessarily blurred and much is missing. I must first apologise, therefore, to those who find here no record of events, actions and soldiers which and whom they believe worthy of record.

Much skill, ingenuity, dedication and courage was displayed by Gunners of this war, recognised frequently by medal-awards; I have felt it invidious to single out such awards when I should have to omit so many and when so many gallant actions inevitably passed unrecognised. Only occasionally have I made exception.

My principal object, in this preface, is to acknowledge the ready help of many individuals, including those who wrote from all parts of Britain, and from as far afield as Swaziland, with narratives and photographs. Many of the latter Mr Ronald Weston of PACE of Charlton, London SE7, reproduced for me with considerable skill. I must particularly mention Maj Warren Bugler, with other members of his strongly-based Regimental Association, on a very notable contribution.

With the ready aid of Brig Lewendon, Miss Wood, Mrs Timbers and Mrs Jones, I researched continually in the Royal Artillery Library. Thanks to Mr Hadfield and Mr Muttett my visits to the Regimental Museum were always profitable. To both RA Institution and to Artillery House I am grateful for much goodwill and encouragement and, in the latter case, for permission to quote freely from the RA Commemoration Book.

I also received much kindness in the Department of Photographs of the Imperial War Museum, where Michael Willis's personal interest, unrivalled knowledge and memory and, may I say, humour made long periods of search positively enjoyable.

I must single-out Maj-Gen B. P. Hughes, not only for his written contributions but also for his unfailing response to cries for help and advice and for most welcome encouragement.

Peter Mead

Glossary

AGRA: Army Group Royal Artillery, reserve, mostly heavier natures of, artillery under the command of an artillery officer responsible to the CCRA (qv).

Airburst: A shell burst, by means of a timed fuse, before it strikes the ground — used against men in the open.

AP (shell): Armour-piercing.

Barrage: Artillery fire, from a number of guns, planned to come down in a linear zone in front of and parallel to the line of forward infantry (cf *Concentration*). Also used to describe a belt of anti-aircraft fire on fixed lines, through which enemy aircraft need to fly en route for their targets.

Bishop: A self-propelled (SP) 25pdr gun, mounted on a *Valentine* tank chassis.

Bombardier, Lance-Bombardier: The Royal Artillery ranks equivalent to *Corporal, Lance-Corporal*.

BRA: Brigadier, Royal Artillery, the senior Artillery officer at an 'Army HQ'.

Breech: The rear end of the *piece* (barrel) of a gun, opened to load the shell, then closed and locked.

Brigade-Major: Staff officer to a Brigade Commander or, in the case of the Royal Artillery, to a *CRA* (qv).

BSM: Battery Sergeant-Major.

Buffer: See *Recoil*.

Carriage: Framework, usually incorporating wheels, for the *piece* or barrel of a gun.

CCRA: Commander, Corps Royal Artillery.

Concentration: Artillery-fire from a number of guns planned to come down upon a particular area (cf *Barrage*).

CPO: Command Post Officer, in charge of a Battery Command Post (cf *GPO*).

CRA: Commander, Royal Artillery, of a Division or comparable body.

Deacon: A self-propelled (SP) 6pdr anti-tank gun, mounted on a 4-wheeled chassis.

DF: Defensive Fire, Artillery fire planned to be called-for and quickly brought down on targets, pre-selected by infantry, on the approaches to their defences (cf *SOS*).

Driving-Band: A band of soft metal around the outside of a shell, near its base. It is engaged by raised metal ridges winding spirally up the inside of the *piece*; the shell is thus given a rotary twist, improving air-penetration, consistency of flight and accuracy.

FOB: Forward Observation Bombardment, an OP party with a landing-party, to control the fire of the guns of HM Ships.

FOO: Forward Observing Officer, accompanying advanced infantry companies or platoons.

FS: Flash-spotting, method of locating enemy guns.

GPO: Gun Position Officer, in charge of a Troop Command Post (cf *CPO*).

HAA: Heavy Anti-aircraft, guns with the role of engaging high-flying enemy aircraft (cf *LAA*).

Havildar: Indian Army rank equivalent to *Sergeant*.

HE (shell): High explosive; a fuze explodes and fragments the shell on impact or at a prearranged height above ground. Designed to cause casualties to personnel.

Howitzer: Field artillery weapon designed to fire at high angle from behind hill-crests etc.

LAA: Light Anti-aircraft, guns with the role of engaging low-flying enemy aircraft.

LCG: Landing Craft — Guns.

LCT: Landing Craft — Tanks (and for self-propelled guns).

LST: Landing Ship — Tanks, larger than *LCT,* with a bow-ramp lowered on to a beach for disembarkation of guns, tanks or other vehicles.

M7: United States self-propelled 3in gun mounted on a Sherman tank chassis.

M10: British 17pdr anti-tank gun mounted on a Sherman tank chassis.

Mike Target: A quick concentration (qv) of fire by all the guns of an artillery regiment.

Naik: Indian Army rank equivalent to *Corporal* or *Bombardier.*

Net: Radio network using a single 'frequency'.

Number 1: Sergeant or Bombardier in charge of one gun detachment.

OP: Observation Post.

OPA: (OP Ack), *Observation Post Assistant,* and deputy, to an observing officer.

Open Sights: Expression to indicate the laying of a gun visually and directly upon an enemy target, rather than by the use of a detached aiming-point, with gun and target remaining out of sight of each other.

Piece: The actual 'barrel' of a gun, at the rear of which the cartridge is exploded to drive the shell out of the muzzle towards the target (c/f *Breech, Carriage, Driving-band*).

Platform: Of gun. A metal wheel placed horizontally on the ground, on which some field guns were brought into action, connected to the centre of the platform and with gun-wheels on its rim, allowing the gun to be quickly swunground to a fresh direction.

Portée: The vehicle upon which certain guns were able not only to travel but also to fire.

-pdr: -pounder, as 6pdr, 25pdr, etc. This refers to the weight of the shell, and is used to describe the gun.

Predictor: An anti-aircraft artillery instrument which, fed with continuous bearings and ranges of target, calculated the latter's course and speed and transmitted to the guns the line and elevation calculated to result in a shellburst at the future position of the target.

Premature: The explosion of a shell within or close to the barrel of a gun, usually with disastrous effects.

Priest: A United States self-propelled 105mm gun on a Grant tank chassis.

Recce: Common army term for 'Reconnoitre' or 'Reconnaissance'.

Recoil: Backward movement of gun in reaction to forward movement of shell induced by explosion of the charge. The backward movement was checked by the *Buffer* and the Piece was returned to its normal position by the *Recuperator.* These two devices were operated by oil and air-filled cylinders.

Recuperator: See *Recoil.*

Register: To record for future artillery-engagement the gun settings required to hit a given target.

REME: The *Royal Electrical and Mechanical Engineers,* the Corps responsible for inspection and repair of Army weapons, vehicles and equipment.

RHQ: Regimental Headquarters.

RSM: Regimental Sergeant Major, senior Warrant-Officer of a Battalion, Regiment of Artillery, etc.

Sexton: Self-propelled 25pdr gun on a Canadian Ram chassis.

SL: Searchlight.

SOS Lines: At night and other inactive periods each battery loads and lays its guns on a given emergency target area selected by the supported infantry. Immediate fire upon this area can be called-for by means of radio transmission or pyrotechnic signal.

SP: Self-propelled, particularly applied to guns incorporating in their carriage (qv) a means of motivation.

SR: Sound-ranging, method of locating enemy guns.

Tiffy: Artificer, specialist in repair, usually of guns.

Trail: Rear portion of a carriage of a gun.

Uncle Target: A quick concentration (qv) of fire by the guns of a Division.

Valentine: Early British tank, the chassis of which was later used for self-propelled 25pdr (*Bishop*) and 17pdr guns.

Victor Target: A quick concentration (qv) of fire by the guns of a Corps.

Waterproofing: Process applied to wheeled and tracked motor vehicles which are likely to be immersed to some extent in landing-operations, to enable their engines and transmissions to remain in action.

Yoke Target: A quick concentration (qv) of fire by the guns of an *Army Group Royal Artillery*.

3
5.5in gun of 1 Medium Regiment in action between Chindwin and Irrawaddy, February 1945. *IWM*

1 The Royal Artillery in 1939

Everyone outside the Royal Artillery agrees that Gunners are extraordinary people and organise their affairs in the most peculiar fashion. So, for the benefit of the non-Gunners, it is necessary to explain something of the Royal Regiment as it was in 1939.

Then, as ever, the Royal Artillery had several separate parts with different functions — though all concerned with guns. The principal divisions were Field Army, Coast and Anti-Aircraft (AA, or in signal terminology of the day 'Ack Ack'). Field army artillery comprised mountain, field, medium, heavy and anti-tank; it also included a 'survey' organisation for the accurate location of our gun positions and, by means of flash-spotting and sound-ranging, of the enemy's guns also. Coast artillery divided itself into close-defence guns, which used automatic sights to measure and set the target-range, and counter-bombardment guns for longer-range shooting. AA artillery included heavy natures (against high-flying aircraft) and light natures (against low-flyers).

Field army artillery had for many years been organised on the basis of the battery, consisting of that number of guns which might conveniently be brought into action and controlled from one command post by voice and megaphone. In 1938 a reorganisation had taken place which, while retaining the battery as the most important fire-unit, divided it into two or three troops of four guns. There were now command posts both at troops and batteries, the former manned by the gun position officer (GPO) and his assistants, telephonists and radio-operators, the latter by the command post officer (CPO) and a similar staff.

A battery might have one or more observation posts (OPs) in areas with visual command over probable target areas. The battery commander (BC) himself, usually, or a representative occasionally, would have his own HQ alongside the infantry commander whom he was supporting and he might also locate forward-observing officers (FOOs) with advanced infantry units or sub-units. Any of these observing officers were ready to initiate the

4
HM King George VI, Colonel-in-Chief of the Royal Artillery from 11 December 1936. *From a portrait in oils by Denis Fildes RA at the Royal Artillery Mess, Woolwich*

5
Garrison Church at Woolwich, HQ of the Royal Artillery, in the 1930s. *PACE, Charlton*

6
Loading the 18pdr Mark V. The No 1 of the gun — the sergeant — is acknowledging an order. Note the prewar service-dress, with the RA lanyard at the shoulder. *Imperial War Museum (IWM)*

7
60pdr medium gun firing during training. *IWM*

battery's engagement of an enemy target by means of fire orders, sent to the GPOs by telephone or radio (or, failing that, by signal-lamp, heliograph, morse-flag or semaphore). Provision was also made for observation of artillery fire by pilots of RAF aeroplanes, who would pass their observations, in code by wireless, to the battery or troop command-posts. GPOs needed to monitor to some extent the fire orders they received, to allow for such matters as uneven intervals between guns or meteorological variations. Their assistants maintained a target location record and marked both gun and target positions on a squared chart on a portable table known as the artillery board.

'Guns' could be either guns or howitzers, the latter weapon designed to fire at high-angle from behind hill crests and the like. It was envisaged that the guns and their detachments would normally, in war, be sited in gun pits and concealed by camouflage netting but digging was rarely practised in peace training. A sergeant commanded each gun detachment and was known as the No 1. The duties of the remainder of the detachment varied with the type of gun but No 3 was usually the layer, responsible for setting the necessary readings on the sight and for directing the gun and sight together so that the latter pointed at a selected aiming point and the former, therefore, at the target. In many natures of guns the layer was also the man who pulled the firing lever. No 4 was usually the loader and higher numbers were responsible for ammunition supply. It was expected that guns would normally fire indirect, at targets out of sight of layers and detachments; they were however provided with the means of engaging targets with direct, visual laying, should necessity arise. The specialist anti-tank gunners expected such direct laying to be their normal lot. When a gun fired, the explosion of the 'Charge' behind the shell drove the latter forward, but also caused the gun itself to 'recoil'. A recoil system, embodied in each gun and actuated by the compression of oil and air, limited the length of recoil and automatically returned the piece (barrel) to its firing position.

By 1939 the bulk of the British field army artillery had been mechanised, in other words tractors and cars had replaced horses and mules; the Quad, the newest field artillery tractor, was destined to be a particularly famous vehicle. Even the Royal Horse Artillery (RHA), the Royal Artillery's corps d'élite, had been mechanised, its role having become that of supporting the tanks and armoured cars which had replaced the horsed cavalry. Only the mountain artillery of the Indian Army retained their mules which carried the 3.7in howitzers in separate loads.

A new gun, the 25-pounder (25pdr), had recently been designed for the field artillery and RHA, to replace both 18pdr and 13pdr guns and 4.5in howitzers. Pending large-scale production, the 18pdr was 'relined' to 25pdr calibre and known as the 18/25pdr. In 1939 and 1940, however, many units were still equipped with the 18pdr and 4.5in. The standard medium artillery equipments were the 6in howitzer and the 60pdr gun; they were gradually to give place to 5.5in and 4.5in guns. Heavy equipments, of which there were few,

were the 8in howitzer and the 6in gun.

For the anti-tank role the 2pdr gun had recently come into service in relatively small numbers; to supplement them, similar Swedish 37mm anti-tank guns had been purchased.

Coast artillery was to be found at the major ports. The 6in Mark VII and 9.2in Mark X were the principal equipments and both were genuine antiques. The 6in gun's 'autosight', provided the state of tide was correctly applied, required the layer merely to lay visually upon the bow-waterline of the target vessel and to fire the gun. The 9.2in gun had follow-the-pointer dials for range and bearing, the incoming information derived from unsophisticated locating instruments. A third gun, the 6pdr Twin, was certainly no antique and was, in any company, remarkable. It could hose-out a stream of shells from two barrels together, in all 70 rounds/min; though it carried an autosight, the layer's function was more usually a direct movement on to the target of the splash-point on the water.

The heavy anti-aircraft (HAA) system of 1939 was based on the 4.5in and 3.7in guns, although many of the 3in guns of 1918 were still perforce in service. Sound locators gave early warning, after which plots were maintained at gun operations rooms (GORs) and information passed to batteries of guns and searchlights. At gun positions spotters used their telescopes-identification to select the target and passed to the predictor detachment its bearing and elevation while the height-finder measured and passed its height. The predictor, already fed with gun and meteorological information, absorbed the incoming target details and from their rate-of-change deduced the target's course and speed and the deflection necessary to allow for it. To

dials on the guns the predictor transmitted the resultant bearings and elevations and, in accordance with the target-height, the requisite fuze setting. By traversing and elevating the gun to keep pointers superimposed on the input-pointers, the gun was thus kept layed in its correct position ahead of the target; it remained only to set the fuze, load and fire the gun. Tactical control was exercised from the GORs. Radar would soon begin to supplement

8
2pdr anti-tank gun. *IWM*

9
6in coast artillery gun, Sheerness. *IWM*

10
6pdr twin coast artillery gun — in any company, remarkable. *IWM*

sort of engagement in which no delay could be brooked.

Gunners sometimes need to be reminded that it is shells, not guns, that kill enemy. The principal form of shell (in 1939) was the 'high explosive' (HE), which, blown to bits among the enemy, distributed those 'bits' at high speed in all directions. For penetration of deep trenches, the armour of tanks or the hulls of ships, forms of 'armour-piercing' (AP) shell were available. Field guns could fire 'smoke' shell to form a screen and thus blind the enemy to the movements of friendly troops. For these, and for other types of shell, a variety of fuzes were available, set by the gun detachments to explode the shells either on impact or shortly before or after impact.

Of the soldiers who manned the guns in 1939, about three-quarters were in the Territorial Army. Some of them were in units recently converted from Yeomanry (Cavalry) to Artillery, a not altogether welcome step for them but one which they accepted cheerfully and efficiently. Particular mention should be made, perhaps, of the so-called 'second-line' TA units which were raised after the Munich conference of 1938; their members volunteered in the unambiguous situation of coming war and their country in danger; the morale and efficiency of these units was seldom less than very high.

These different branches of the Regiment seemed to demand different qualities — the hot-blooded courage required of an anti-tank gunner a great contrast to the cool skill and detachment of the predictor number or the coast artilleryman's need to preserve alertness and quickness of reaction after months of operational inactivity. One factor was common to almost all — the guns — and it was this factor, more often than not, which inspired the heights of courage and concentration.

Infantry and other regiments have battle honours but, since 1833, the Royal Artillery has borne the single honour, *Ubique* — Everywhere — indicating its presence wherever the army goes.

This book can do no more than select a few incidents and a few engagements of World War 2 and relate the Gunners' part in them. Let it not be thought, by those who read, that the Artillery was not, as in the past and as in the future, *Ubique*.

11
Mobile 3.7in Mark IIIA HAA gun, with tractor. *IWM*

12
Vickers Predictor. *IWM*

sound locators for early warning; future models were to be used in place of spotters' telescopes and height-finders to produce target information for the predictors, but those days were still ahead.

The standard light anti-aircraft (LAA) gun, against the low-flying aircraft, was the Swedish 40mm Bofors, though many batteries were equipped with 20mm Oerlikons or Hispanos or even with twin machine guns. On the Bofors two layers followed the path of the target, one for elevation, the other (using a deflection sight) for line. A predictor had been designed for the LAA role but many believed it to be an unacceptable delaying factor in the

2 Phoney War to Blitzkrieg

On 1 September 1939 Germany's invasion of Poland set in motion World War 2. A British Expeditionary Force, under Gen Lord Gort, crossed the Channel and formed up on the left of the French armies. As CIGS, Chief of the Imperial General Staff, head of the British Army, Lord Gort was succeeded by a very notable Gunner, Gen Sir Edmund Ironside.

Instead of the expected German attack on the West the 'Phoney War' set in, distinguished by little more than patrolling, leaflet-dropping from aircraft, German submarine attacks on British shipping and a peace proposal from Hitler. The BEF dug defences on the French frontier with Belgium (which, like Holland, was still neutral) and carried out training.

In early April 1940 Hitler suddenly invaded Denmark and Norway. British help to the latter was 'too little, too late'; although a base was temporarily

13
24 Field Regiment's last parade at Waterloo Barracks, Aldershot, as it moves off to war, September 1939. Note the Morris tractor.
Lt-Col J. F. Willcocks

14
8in gun of 1 Heavy Regiment, concealed in a French farmyard, October 1939
IWM

established in northern Norway, the danger of a German attack on France made reinforcement impossible. Dissatisfaction with the conduct of the war was voiced in the Commons and resulted in the resignation of the British Prime Minister, Neville Chamberlain, and his succession by that great war leader, Winston Churchill.

The French placed great faith in the strong defences of their Maginot Line, which extended from the Swiss to Belgian frontier. It was considered likely that the Germans would try to outflank this line by advancing through Holland and Belgium, in spite of their neutrality, and it was planned in such event to forestall them by moving quickly forward to the line of the River Dyle. The Germans moved into Holland and Belgium on 10 May and the Allied plans were set in train.

The 10th Field Regiment (CO Lt-Col H. J. Parham) was engaged in unit training, well to the west of their winter quarters, when the balloon went up. After a smooth drive forward, its batteries were in position on the Dyle on 13 May. Thirty-six hours later they were firing harassing fire against the oncoming enemy, followed next day by observed shooting against assaulting infantry. On the evening of 15 May this regiment achieved a success which may have been a minor one but which was to prove of later significance. Col Parham, in an account of his regiment's operations, wrote:

'I was rung up from the right OP, overlooking Wavre, by M who said his look-out man (actually his signaller) had spotted Boche tanks camouflaging themselves on *our* side of a wood! The inference was that if some were *there*, there were probably lots more inside so I ordered a regimental concentration, all exactly as per miniature range, and at zero hour, some ten minutes later, we put 500 rounds at rate intense into the wood without any preliminary ranging. It was a grand crash and excited chuckles down the OP wire confirmed that we had struck a winner. That wood blazed for several hours with big black columns of smoke indicating petrol fires. A good effort on the part of an alert OP.'

15

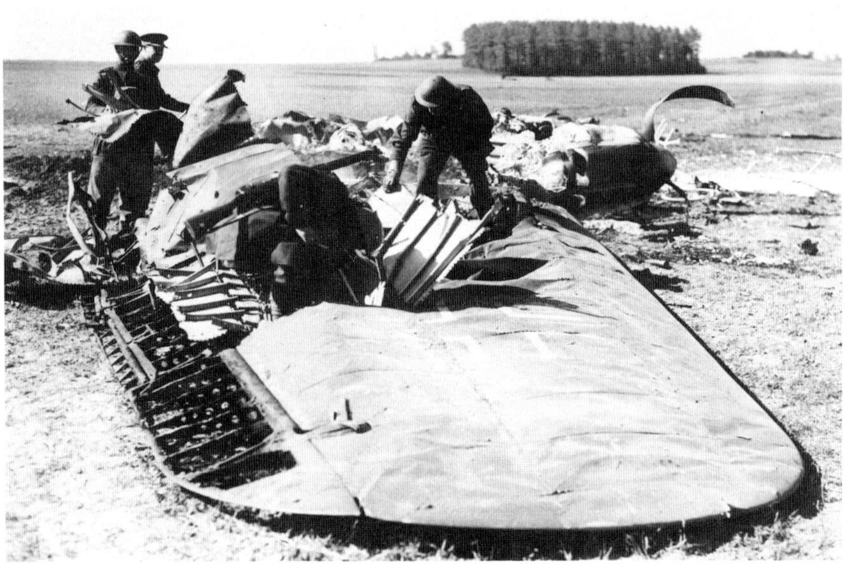

15
Heinkel bomber shot down by British AA fire near Tournai, May 1940 *IWM*

16

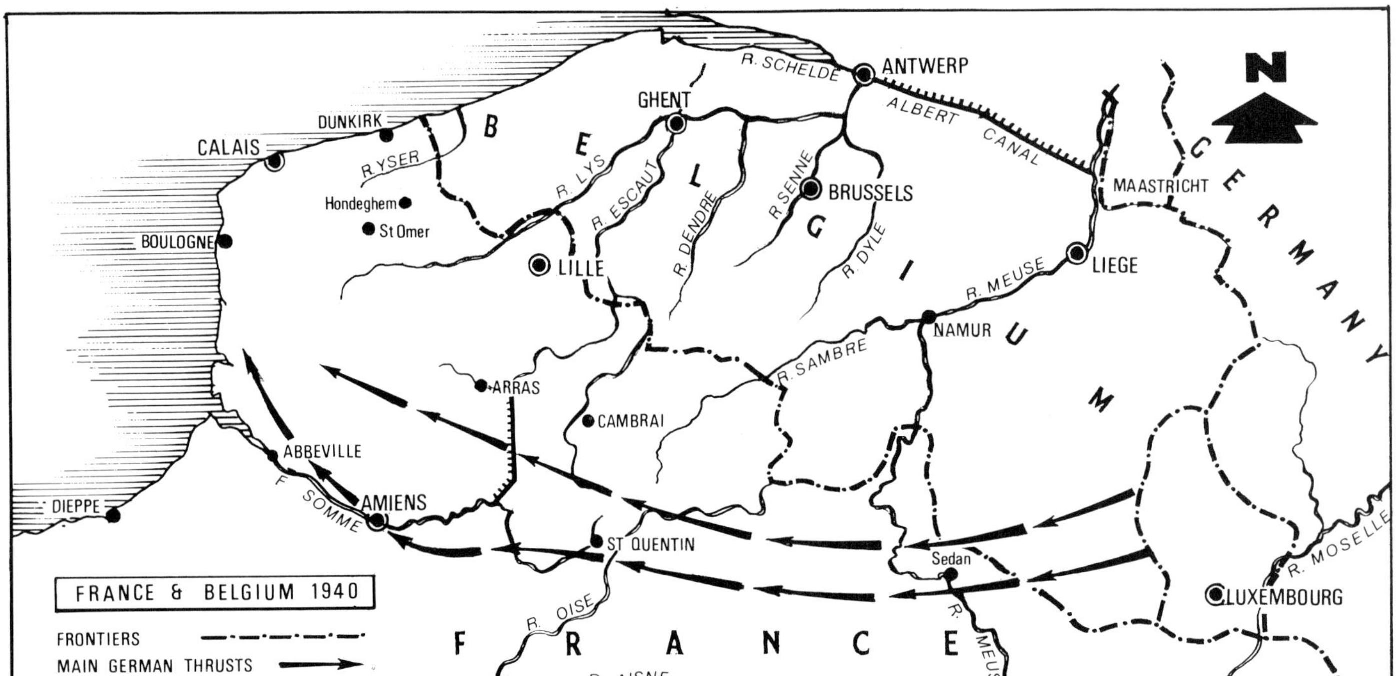

16
France and Belgium, 1940

The term 'regimental concentration' implied the simultaneous fire of all 24 25pdrs of the Regiment — a fairly intricate operation in those days, involving not only artillery boards but also trigonometrical checks. Ten minutes was good going!

That night began the British withdrawal which, through monstrous traffic jams, under spectacular but strangely ineffective dive-bombing attacks, in an intense fog of war, brought the BEF back to the Dunkirk beaches by 30 May.

The 10th Field Regiment's regimental concentration was not typical of the use of field artillery in this campaign. Artillery, like other forms of support, was in short supply and when things are in short supply they tend to be parcelled-out in small packages to many bidders. On 22 May, for example, south of St Omer, the seven available guns of 392nd Battery of 98th Field Regiment were dispatched to seven separate bridges over the canal, sometimes but not always with a little infantry protection, to prevent or delay the enemy's crossing. One gun detachment survived and held back the enemy for three days before being relieved by the French. Two other detachments delayed the enemy for several hours and, in each case, lost their gun to enemy artillery fire as they were withdrawing. A third got away. The remaining three detachments were quickly overrun.

On 26 May 1940, at and around the village of Hondeghem, a remarkable delaying action was fought by K Battery of 5th Regiment, RHA, and a small detachment from a Searchlight Regiment. K Battery was commanded by Maj Rawdon Hoare; it was equipped with veteran Mark II 18pdrs of World War 1 vintage which were, nevertheless, not unsuited to the action which ensued. Hoare sited D Troop three miles north of the village with an OP in Hondeghem church tower and F Troop under Capt N. B. C Teacher,

with machine gunners and riflemen, in the village itself. Two of F Troop's guns were sited to cover the probable German approach routes from the south and east, the other two retained in the northern half of the village. Three road-blocks were prepared and covered by fire.

Early on the 27th enemy tanks appeared on the southern outskirts, were engaged by the outlying guns but overran them in a 10-minute battle. This was a heavy blow and enemy tanks and infantry now began to move through the village. The OP in the church, however, harassed this movement and all such movements for the rest of the morning, after which enemy artillery began to shell the church

17
The concealment of a British 2pdr anti-tank gun — probably of 51 Anti-tank Regiment south-west of Abbeville, on about 26 May 1940. *IWM*

18
18/25pdr of 51st Highland Division in action south-west of Abbeville, about 26 May 1940. *IWM*

19
Panorama by Lt-Col H. J. Parham, 27 May 1940. Panorama-sketching was an OP-skill taught to all Gunner officers; Parham used it frequently, throughout the war, to record important information. *Mrs Barbara Parham*

17

18

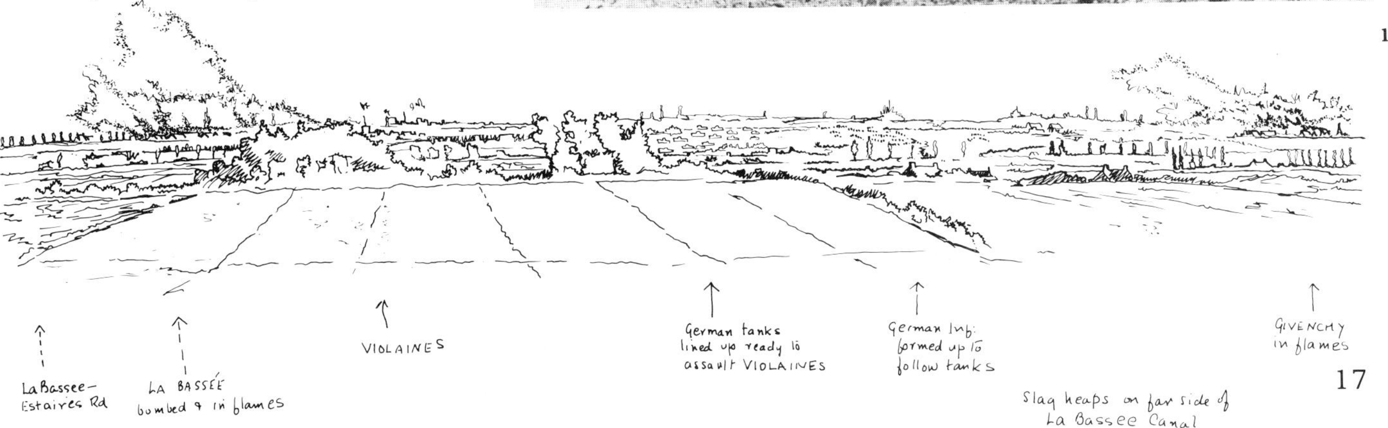

19

20
'If only . . .' Photographed from his following car by General Erwin Rommel as he advanced along the road to Arras about a week before Dunkirk. British artillery scores a near-miss. *IWM*

21
Hondeghem — RSM R. Millard, then BSM, K Battery. *Royal Artillery Charitable - Fund*

tower. The two 18pdrs inside the village started to engage the enemy as soon as they appeared, man-handling the guns along the street to suitable positions, firing and withdrawing before the enemy could retaliate. The enemy got a machine gun into the battery cookhouse where it was promptly destroyed (with the battery breakfast) by one of the 18pdrs, while the other demolished a farmhouse which concealed another machine gun. German infantry advanced to grenade-throwing range, but casualties among the two gun detachments were few and those to the attackers considerable — some from gunfire and others from rifle-fire from upper windows.

More and more German machine guns were filtered forward into the village, however, and the guns had constantly to be moved. D Troop, from the slopes of Mount Cassel, brought down defensive fire 50 yards south of the church which provided some respite; soon, however, three D Troop guns were put out of action by enemy artillery fire. Ammunition in Hondeghem was running low and at 4.15pm withdrawal was ordered to the village of Ste Sylvestre, two miles to the north-west.

At Ste Sylvestre the enemy was found in possession, but the Gunners were joined by a small party of riflemen of the Royal Army Service Corps. A body of German infantry was expelled from a graveyard by the unusual expedient (for Gunners) of a bayonet charge. The guns were then brought into action and expended their remaining ammunition. One of F Troop's two guns, with its tractor, was destroyed, however, by a German gun which used similar tactics to that of F Troop in Hondeghem.

Darkness was falling. Having destroyed their last gun, the detachments piled into the remaining vehicles, which were driven rapidly through the village, the German defences and a British minefield to rejoin their battery. They had held up the enemy for 12 hours.

Dunkirk lay ahead, however, whence the BEF could evacuate no heavy weapons or equipment. After Dunkirk there was a brief campaign in north-western France, the German occupation of Paris and the French capitulation. Britain was isolated and the Battle of Britain soon to begin.

A story of personal courage and determination may, however, here be told. It started on 27 May, 18 miles south of Dunkirk, when 367th Battery of 140th Field Regiment fought a long battle against tanks until its ammunition was expended. By then it was surrounded and on the next day its survivors were captured, one of these being a young West Countryman, Gnr William John Martin, a Quad driver.

In November 1940 news came that Martin had reached Gibraltar and on 17 February 1941 he reported back to his Regiment, now in Bournemouth. The CO, Lt-Col H. G. R. Brooks, questioned him and, on the following day, wrote a report of which an extract was sent to the author from Swaziland by Maj G. L. Somerwill, who was then in 140th Regiment.

'With his fellow prisoners belonging to 367 Field Battery he (Martin) marched south east to Doullens, St Pol and Cambrai, where they were put on a train. Some time later in the darkness whilst stationary at Hirson on the frontier he succeeded in jumping off the train and got away. This was his first escape.

'He succeeded in obtaining civilian clothing and remained at large for two days. He was then recaptured, taken before the Commandant who not unnaturally, seeing that he was in civilian clothes, took him for a spy. He was interrogated by a French captain, who apparently succeeded in convincing the Commandant that he was an escaped prisoner and Gnr Martin was put into the prison camp, where he remained for five weeks with some 300 French prisoners. At the end of this period he managed to escape for the second time.

'He managed to make his way as far as Suxanne. There he was captured and taken to Épernay. It was then discovered that he had escaped before. He was set to work with some French prisoners and remained there three weeks at the end of which time he succeeded in escaping for the third time.

'From there he made his way to Marseilles, hiding by day and living on fruit. This took him about six weeks. At Marseilles he was arrested and put in a concentration camp by the French owing to the fact that he had no papers to identify himself. After ten days he, with sixty others, succeeded in escaping from the camp and managed to stow away in a ship bound for Oran. This was his fourth escape.

'From this time on he planned and worked in association with Private Philip Lindsay of the 1st Battalion The Black Watch. After 14 days in Oran, where he spent his time in hiding and surreptitiously making enquiries as to how he could get to Casablanca, he was discovered by a French gendarme

and arrested and put away in jail. He was then sent to a concentration camp. After a week in that camp he succeeded in getting away. He and Private Lindsay eventually succeeded in smuggling themselves aboard a boat to Casablanca where they immediately managed to get in touch with the American Consul who treated them with the greatest of kindness and endeavoured to help them get away, communicating with the British consulate at Lisbon. They eventually got away on a Portuguese sugar boat from which they were shipped on to a British destroyer in the Straits of Gibraltar.

'Gunner Martin landed at Gourock on 14 December 1940 and was sent to the RA Depot at Woolwich.'

A note on the unit copy of this report states simply 'Awarded DCM (Distinguished Conduct Medal) March 1941'.

22
Bofors LAA gun, with detachment who claimed 10 enemy aircraft destroyed in five weeks. Detachment and gun were rescued from Cherbourg and arrived at Southampton 18 June. *IWM*

3 Defence of the Realm

The evacuation from Dunkirk of the British Expeditionary Force, and of elements of the French Army, was, as Churchill was careful to point out at the time, no victory. It represented a magnificent achievement by the RAF, in keeping the Luftwaffe clear of the beachhead, by the Royal Navy, in evacuating so many in such hazardous conditions, and by the Army in maintaining its resistance and covering the evacuation. The great mass of the Army's heavy weapons and equipment had, however, to be abandoned on the continent, among them 600 anti-tank guns, 1,000 field guns and 50 heavier guns. Perhaps the most urgent task of all, for those who received, reorganised and retasked the returning soldiers, was to rearm the Gunners.

The main sources of guns for this purpose were the Royal Navy and the USA. The former produced 6in, 4.7in and 4in guns, removed long since from scrapped warships and some reputedly discovered under a mountain of coal. The Americans produced several hundred 75mm guns of three separate types — French guns of 1897, British 18pdrs converted to 75mm calibre and more modern American artillery. Ammunition for all these guns was in short supply.

An early German invasion attempt was expected and high priority was given to the beach and coast defences. Coast artillery had hitherto been found only at the major ports; naval guns were now mounted at many smaller ports and on vulnerable stretches of coastline. Supplementing these were so-called 'defence batteries' of the Royal Artillery, employed in the coast defence role but equipped with mobile

23
Well-concealed 6in coast gun emplacement, Southwold. *IWM*

24
'Emergency' battery of 4in naval guns at Blundellsands, Liverpool, manned by 385 Field Battery. *IWM*

23

24

guns. In quite a different category was the concentration of 'cross-channel' guns in the Dover area, including eventually 9.2in, 14in and 15in coast guns (the 14in guns manned by Royal Marines) and 'super-heavy' railway guns; the role of all these guns was to harass enemy attempts to run shipping through the straits.

Hitler indeed intended to invade, and the middle of August 1940 was his first planned date for that exploit. That it was postponed progressively to September, October, the following spring and eventually *sine die* was, of course, primarily due to the Luftwaffe's failure to defeat RAF's Fighter Command, an essential preliminary to any invasion. The Army's Anti-aircraft Command, led throughout the war by Gen Sir Frederick Pile, was always closely linked to Fighter Command. AA batteries, however, although radar now helped with early warning of approaching aircraft, still lacked the means of applying accurate fire (particularly by night) to a target flying fast and making changes of course, speed and height. Their main value was in breaking up large bomber forces for easier attack by fighters and as a deterrent, a harassment and (when sufficient ammunition was expended) a morale-booster for the civilian population.

Sunday, 15 September, was an historic day in the Battle of Britain, when the Luftwaffe launched over 500 aircraft and were resoundingly defeated. Chief honours belonged to the RAF, of course, but the following extract from the contemporary AA Command publication *Roof over Britain* (used with the permission of Her Majesty's Stationery Office) gives an artillery view of the day.

'At about 2.30 pm the first of two great waves of enemy planes, each more than 150 strong, crossed the coast between Dover and Dungeness and thrust towards the Thames estuary. Less than a hundred of them managed to elude the fighter net and reach the south-eastern outskirts of London. Eight minutes after crossing the coast it was apparent that they were headed

Big guns near Dover

25
'Boche Buster' An 18in railway gun of the 1914-18 war, back again in 1942 with 11 Super-Heavy Battery at Bishopsbourne. *IWM*

26
15in coast gun at Wanstone Battery, Dover, 519 Coast Regiment.
RA Regimental Museum

27
Command Post of 303 HAA
Battery, Hayes Common, Kent
— note height finder on the
left. *IWM*

28
90cm searchlight. *IWM*

bombers. The foremost Dornier
swerved and dived away, a long plume
of smoke trailing from its cockpit. From
the engines of the second came thin
wisps of white smoke that grew to a
cloud. The formation turned away
from the wall of bursts towards the
Medway, climbing steadily and
spreading widely, like the fingers of an
outstretched hand. One of them
exploded with a direct hit, and a string
of flaming fragments fell towards the
river. More and more gun stations took
up the action: there was an infernal
crescendo of sound. For half a minute
— how disproportionately short these
significant battles are — the Dorniers
pressed on in formation. Then, over
Dartford, the close wedge was broken,
and as the bombers scattered to avoid
the bursting shells, Hurricanes and
Spitfires, diving out of the sun, did
execution.

'Meanwhile to the south-west of
Chatham a second wave of Heinkels
was similarly faltering under intense
gunfire. Long before the Medway was
reached its ranks had degenerated into
a straggling line, widely dispersed.

'For some minutes the cloudy sky
above the Isle of Grain was the setting
for high drama. The routed Dorniers of
the first wave were staggering about in
dog-fights, the sky a wild medley of
twisting aircraft. The white discs of
parachutes hung in the air. Over
Chatham the guns still held the stage,
and the Heinkels of the second wave
rocked and jinked as they tried to run
the gauntlet of the barking inner guns
and the cruisers in the river. The
leading Heinkel, caught in a salvo of
3.7-inch shells with its bomb-load still

straight for the Chatham guns. There
was not long to wait. Distant thuds
came in quick succession as the West
Malling guns engaged them. A curtain
of white puffs, remote and unreal,
shrouded the toy-like specks. One of
them fell away trailing black smoke.
Now they could be identified through
binoculars, about 40 Dornier 215's, in
close arrowhead formation, with their
fighters, flying at 18,000 feet and
250 m.p.h.

'The staff officers who provided the
material for this story were watching
from one of the old forts of Chatham,
built to repel an earlier invasion which
never came. The bombers came
steadily on. The range shortened. From
the sunlit town there was neither noise
nor movement.

'Then the outer gun stations went
into action. The black bursts of the first
salvoes sprang up among the leading

in the racks, blew to pieces at 19,000 feet. Almost at the same instant another Heinkel, hit in the cockpit and engines, fell flaming down towards Dartford Park. Thirty seconds later, over the Isle of Sheppey, the guns shot away the tail of a third machine, which dived 5000 feet into the sea and disappeared entirely. The guns had shot down three raiders in less than three minutes.

'Not far away the Bofors gunners engaged a Dornier flying fast and low towards the sea. Repeated hits were scored, the target danced antics in the air, both engines caught fire, and he turned over and fell towards the sea. The air at this time was full of the crumps of bursting salvoes, the whine of falling shell splinters, the uproar of engines. And as the London batteries engaged, the din was multiplied.

'A third wave of enemy approached, mainly Dorniers, at slightly over 16,000 feet. This was the last mass-formation attack of the day. It was not a mass formation for long. It was quickly scattered by the guns, and, while out of range of the majority of batteries, the enemy turned away westwards to meet the Nemesis of further fighter squadrons.

'In the mopping-up actions, when the returning enemy came within range at all, two more Dorniers and a Messerschmitt 109 fell to the heavy guns and two Dorniers to the light anti-aircraft batteries. It is not possible to detail all the incidents of that crowded half-hour, which, of course, seemed like hours of battle to the people who took part. A fugitive Dornier appeared out of the clouds over a Bofors position, to be shot down in flames only 500 yards from the gun-pit. A Messerschmitt, its tail shot away at 15,000 feet, whined down to shatter itself in a rural churchyard. Another Dornier, already hit in the port engine, blundered over Chatham at 5000 feet. As the 4.5-inch bursts sprang up beside it pieces of wing and fuselage broke away from it. Four occupants baled out and were captured by cheering civilians who raced across the fields, while the pilotless bomber, skimming the roof tops, buried itself in a cottage garden.

'Shortly before five o'clock the gunners of a cargo vessel steaming down the river hit a Heinkel with their twelve-pounder at 200 yards range, and saw it crash into the mudflats on the Essex side of the river.

'During these late engagements cloud almost completely covered the sky and visibility grew gradually worse. It was under these conditions that the last action of the day took place. At 3.15 pm a single Dornier 215 dived from low cloud, cracking away with its machine-gun at the streets of an estuary town. At 3000 feet a Bofors opened up and brought it down flaming — a red exclamation mark to close the story of a memorable day.'

By the end of October daylight attacks on the aerodromes and on London had virtually ceased and night raids began to be directed upon provincial cities. Night-fighter tactics had been developing and searchlight batteries had an important part to play, to trap the

29
3in AA gun during night raid on Cardiff, August 1940 — one enemy aircraft 'confirmed', another 'probable'. *IWM*

30
75 HAA Battery in action near Dover, October 1940 *IWM*

29

30

raider in a cone of three beams and to keep it there, a fresh beam taking over as each one was outranged. In 1941 searchlight batteries began to be equipped with their own special radar set, with the name 'Elsie'.

For all these steadily increasing defences extra manpower was needed, but manpower was also needed in the Middle East. The Home Guard helped, available only in off-duty periods from their civilian jobs but organised into watches to man AA, Coast and 'Defence' battery weapons. The principal solution, however, especially for AA, proved to be woman-power, girls of the Auxiliary Territorial Service (ATS) being employed not only for administrative, but for operational AA duties on fire-control instruments such as telescopes-identification, predictors, height-finders, radar and plotting tables. In due course they operated AA searchlights too, involving deployment in field conditions, guard duties (in which it was thought suitable to provide them with pick-helves rather than firearms) and their reinforcement by a single male soldier on each site to 'swing' the generator starting-handle. The ATS experiment, described by Churchill as one of the greatest ever tried in the British Army, was a resounding success.

AA Targets, 1940

31
Heinkel 111s. *IWM*
32
Dornier shot down near Victoria, London. *IWM*

The first 'Mixed' HAA regiment opened fire on 1 November 1941 and, exactly a week later, at Newcastle, another mixed regiment downed its first bomber. In May 1942 the AA ATS suffered their first fatal operational casualty, Pte N. Caveney, a predictor number, being hit by a bomb splinter. As she collapsed a spotter took her place and the engagement continued without a break. The girls dearly wished to be regarded as Gunners. So indeed they were, by all but their parent service which adamantly opposed any apparent movement towards a 'take-over'. Permitted to be worn, however, was the RA lanyard, the grenade badge above the pocket and, by sergeants, the cannon badge above their stripes.

Among the predictor numbers of 137th (Mixed) HAA Regiment was Violette Szabo, wife of a 'Free French' soldier. She was a keen and efficient 'Gunner' and popular with her fellows. She left in order to have a baby, a daughter, and her husband was at that point killed at El Alamein. Later she volunteered for a mission of great danger in German-occupied France, into which she parachuted in 1944. The citation for her George Cross continues:

'In her execution of the delicate researches entailed she showed great presence of mind and astuteness. She was twice arrested by the German security authorities, but each time managed to get away. Eventually, however, with other members of her group, she was surrounded by the Gestapo in a house in the south-west of France.

'Resistance appeared hopeless, but

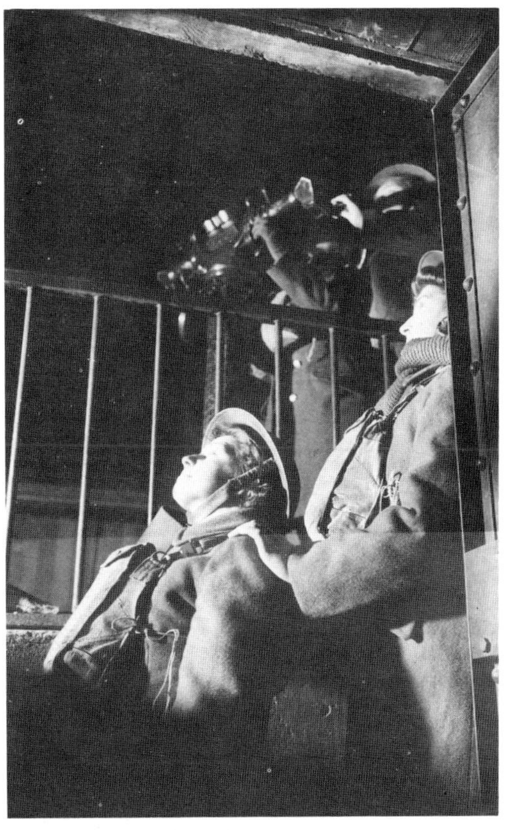

The Gunner ATS

33
450 (Mixed) HAA Battery, Wormwood Scrubs site, London, Spotters. *IWM*
34
450 Battery — plotting table. *IWM*
35
439 (Mixed) HAA Battery, Walthamstow, London, April 1942, Corporal Mary Churchill meets her parents. *IWM*

36
Violette Szabo, George Cross. *Press Association Ltd*

37
Maunsell Fort. A number of these, named after their designer, were set up in Thames (as here) and Mersey to close gaps in the defences.
IWM

38
The Bofors — principal weapon against the low-level attacks.
Brig B. Chichester-Cooke

Mme Szabo, seizing a Sten gun and as much ammunition as she could carry, barricaded herself in part of the house and, exchanging shot for shot with the enemy, killed or wounded several of them. By constant movement she avoided being cornered and fought until she dropped exhausted. She was arrested and had to undergo solitary confinement. She was then continuously and atrociously tortured, but never by word or deed gave away any of her acquaintances or told the enemy anything of any value. She was ultimately executed. Mme Szabo gave a magnificent example of courage and steadfastness.'

The Royal Artillery may indeed be proud that Violette Szabo served in its ranks.

Radar, by 1942, was giving adequate early warning of enemy aircraft approaching at high or medium altitudes; below this there was a gap, where warning was short and identification too late. The Luftwaffe took advantage of this gap to stage a series of high-speed attacks by fighter-bombers at very low altitudes, mostly against non-military targets near the south-east and south coasts. These attacks were essentially a challenge to our LAA artillery (already depleted by the demands of Africa and the need to arm merchant vessels) and for 12 months a very special battle was waged.

Maj-Gen B. P. Hughes, who was in 1943 a brigadier of the operations staff of AA Command, explains the measures taken to conduct this battle. 'The most important step taken was to connect the low-looking radar directly both to the fighter-aircraft's dispersals and to the LAA Troops; this, of course, provided only "raw" information, unfiltered and unidentified, but it was coupled with a rule prohibiting friendly aircraft from crossing the coast below 1,000 feet and giving the guns freedom to engage below 500 feet without recognition.

'Ultimately 543 40mm guns were deployed on the "Fringe targets", reinforced by 304 20mm Oerlikons manned by the RAF Regiment, 506 Vickers twin .5mm machine guns and 340 2-inch rocket-projectors.

'There was, however, still scope for improvement in ways of alerting the LAA defences. The strain of continuous manning throughout the hours of daylight, while gazing into a mixture of haze and sun over the sea, called for frequent reliefs and physical exercises to maintain alertness. But it was in the sphere of "local warning" that the greatest advances were made; Brigadier E. S. Lindsay of 2nd AA Group was foremost in devising these, which included detached visual OPs, connected to the guns by radio, and a simple, but most profitable, system of colour code to indicate the direction of approach.

'As a result of these improved arrangements the reinforced gun defences showed a marked improvement in performance during the autumn of 1942, 34 aircraft casualties being caused between October and January. There was a slight drop in the number of attacks during the bad weather of February 1943, and then the guns really started hitting, 13 aircraft casualties being inflicted in 12 attacks. The great day, however, was on 30 May when of 15 FW190s which

Training, 1940-42

39
229 Field Battery on an exercise in Nottinghamshire in August 1940. Note the 'Quad' tractor, a very famous and successful vehicle. *IWM*

40
Maj-Gen (then Brigadier) F. W. H. (Ambrose) Pratt, a great trainer of artillerymen. *From a 1940 sketch by S. Morse Brown, photograph by PACE, Charlton, courtesy Royal Artillery Charitable Fund*

flew into Torbay 6 were put straight into the sea and, of another 20 which attacked Frinton, 4 were brought to an untimely end. With 3 more destroyed, 1 probably destroyed, and 3 hit and damaged on the next three days the German Air Force had had enough and the attacks ceased completely.

'From first to last the guns had destroyed 56 aircraft with another 8 probably destroyed and 49 damaged, an overall casualty rate of 9.2%. During the last three months the German casualties from guns had risen to 15.7%, 9.9% having been destroyed or probably destroyed over the targets. To these losses must be added the casualties inflicted by the aircraft of Fighter Command — an overall figure of 51 destroyed, 4 probably destroyed and 25 damaged over the whole period, and it will be clear, as it was to the Germans, that low altitude attacks on the coasts of England had been unmistakably defeated.'

While Fighter and AA Commands battled with the Luftwaffe, the Field Force formations of the British Army, strategically placed to react to invasion attempts, trained steadily for the time when they would return to the offensive on the continent of Europe or elsewhere. Training is an essential part of war and those who imaginatively and thoroughly prepared their units and soldiers for the test of battle were as

much battle-winners as those who, when the time came, led them in the field. A notable trainer and Gunner personality was Brig Ambrose Pratt, who in 1940 and 1941 was CCRA (the senior Gunner) of X Corps — at Scotch Corner, Yorkshire. Brig John Daniell, who at that time was on Ambrose Pratt's staff, writes of him:

'He had little use for the Staff College, Horse Artillery or ceremonial, though of course recognising that they had their uses in the right place. Everything had to be down to earth, and a test seemingly just beyond the capabilities of those being tested.

'Hey, what's this? Turn out the Guard!' Just a visit by munition workers to 243 Field Battery, Downpatrick, Northern Ireland, January 1942. *IWM*

Field-Marshal Lord Ironside (left), CIGS from August 1939 to June 1940, with Lt-Gen H. R. S. Massy, GOC-in-C XI Corps. Massy played a big part in establishing the Air OP organisation, as is later described. *IWM*

'I had the worst rocket of my service from Ambrose when on a Corps HQ exercise, no units involved except on paper, an imaginary regiment due to arrive somewhere in the middle of the night. I made the necessary paper record and went to bed, to be awakened by Ambrose asking why I wasn't out meeting the imaginary regiment (where he himself had been).

'He somehow got permission to fire live shells over a peaceful Yorkshire countryside, the target area being the incoming tide on the supposed enemy landing beaches and this was practised by the least skilful of the Corps artillery regiments before they were allowed to go to camp for proper practice shooting. One fully loaded railway coal wagon was the only casualty I remember.

But his best effort in those days was when an only partially trained TA regiment was sent to join the Corps artillery. He first satisfied himself that the potential was there and then set them to work out a barrage with the help of air photos, to be fired live on to a reasonably empty bit of country but, as usual, the shells would pass over inhabited areas. At zero-hour (7am on a foggy morning) he took me and his intelligence officer, John Sharp, in his car to where he said the leading infantry would be.

'Didn't John and I duck when the

Field-Marshal Lord Alanbrooke, C-in-C Home Forces 1940 to 1941, CIGS 1941 to 1945

Arthur Bryant wrote that he 'carried a burden of sustained responsibility greater than that borne by any other soldier in our history'.

43
With (left) Gen Sir Ronald Adam and (right) Maj-Gen A. E. Percival, on an exercise in the north of England, 1940. *IWM*

44
With (standing centre) Gen Sir Bernard Montgomery, near El Alamein, Egypt, 1942. *IWM*

first shell came over — but not Ambrose. The resulting uplift to the morale of that particular regiment was terrific and it never looked back; I read of it distinguishing itself later in the war and traced it back to that morning.'

In June 1941 Germany invaded Russia; from that moment Britain ceased to be a beleaguered fortress but rather a base, vigilantly protected against both sea and air attacks, from which the forces of liberation were in due course to be launched across the Channel.

Gen Sir Alan Brooke, later Field-Marshall Lord Alanbrooke, a Gunner by trade and upbringing, had commanded II Corps of the BEF in France. On return to England, he became Commander-in-Chief (C-in-C) Home Forces, responsible for the defence of the country against invasion. But at the end of 1941 he became CIGS and Chairman of the Chiefs of Staff Committee, offices which he held with distinction for the rest of the war.

4 Mediterranean Shores

To the people of Britain, acutely aware of their isolation and of the strength of their enemies, the most heartening event of the hard winter of 1940-41 was Gen Wavell's sudden assault from Egypt, where he had some 30,000 soldiers, upon an Italian invasion force of about 80,000.

The Italians had established themselves, about 50 miles within the Egyptian frontier, in a line of fortified camps extending some 20 miles inland from Sidi Barrani on the Mediterranean coast. Wavell's plan, prepared with the greatest secrecy, was to overwhelm two of the inland camps and sweep round to the sea west of Sidi Barrani, while 7th Armoured Division (the Desert Rats to be) covered the south flank. The 4th Indian Division moved out with its artillery on 8 December 1940; by 7.15am next day the first camp was under artillery fire and by 10.40 it had fallen. The divisional artillery then moved north to assist in the capture of the second camp by 4pm. By early afternoon on the 10th the exits from Sidi Barrani had been closed. Lt-Gen R. N. O'Connor, Commander of the Western Desert Force, set 7th Armoured Division to the pursuit.

The Italians left garrisons in the ports of Bardia and Tobruk but their main army concentrated east of Benghazi; O'Connor's aim was nothing short of its destruction. To that end he sent Maj-Gen M. O'Moore Creagh and his 7th Armoured Division south-west across the desert to cut the coast road south of Benghazi. Creagh sent on ahead, under Lt-Col J. F. B. Combe of the 11th Hussars, a small column consisting of 2nd Battalion the Rifle Brigade, the armoured cars of 11th Hussars and King's Dragoon Guards, C

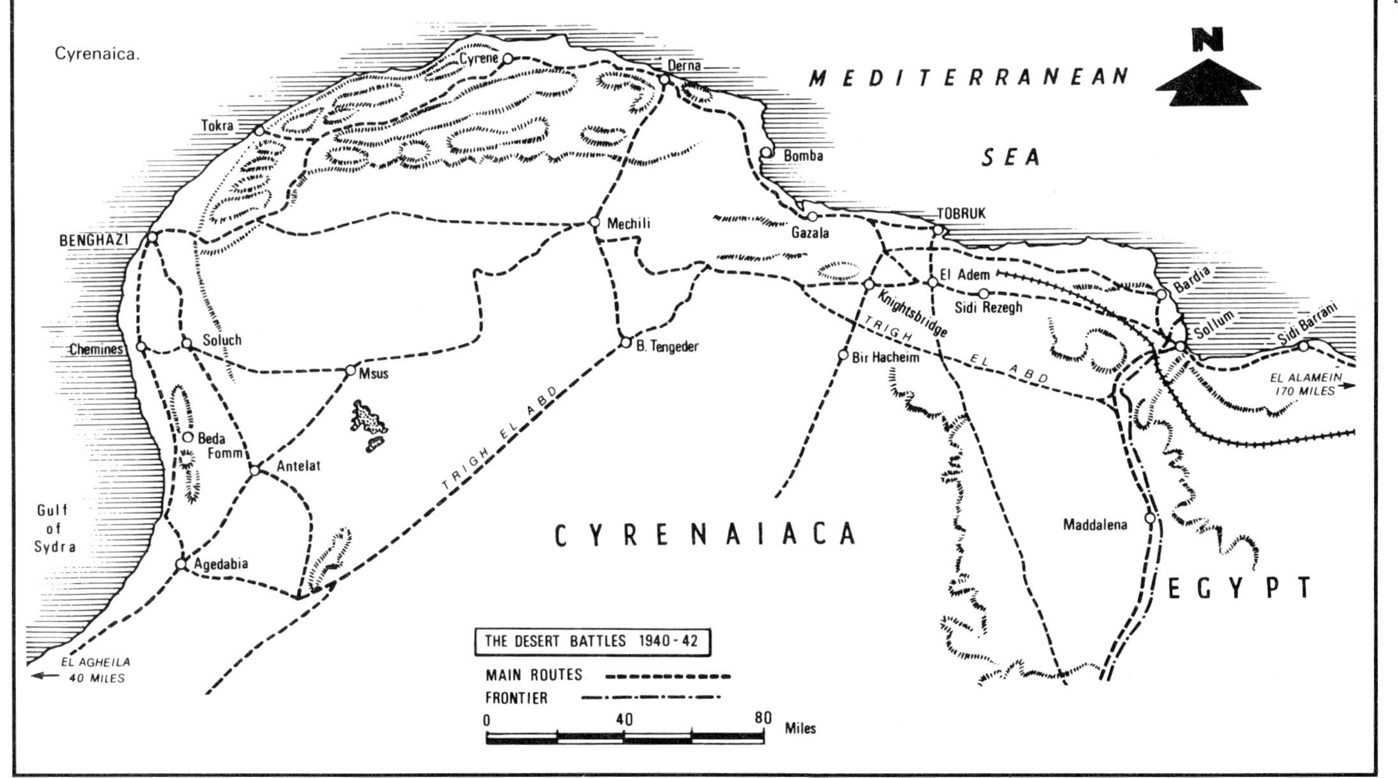

45
The Desert Battles 1940-42.

46
6in howitzer of 7 Medium Regiment firing into the Bardia defences, December 1940. *IWM*

47
25pdr in action against the Tobruk defences, January 1941. *IWM*

48
Field battery command post outside Tobruk, January 1941. *IWM*

Battery of 4th Regiment, RHA (with 25pdr field guns) and the 1st and part of the 2nd Anti-tank Battery of 106th Regiment (Lancashire Yeomanry), RHA. This last Regiment was armed with 37mm Bofors anti-tank guns.

At midday on 5 February the small column debouched on the north to south road, 60 miles south of Benghazi and about 10 miles south-west of the village of Beda Fomm which gave its name to the subsequent battle. Nine of the anti-tank guns were available, mostly kept 'portée', that is mounted on their transport vehicle and ready to fire therefrom; they were sited under cover of the small sandhills which abounded in that area.

The first Italians appeared that afternoon and were easily dealt with. After a quiet night and Italian reconnaissances next morning in which the anti-tank guns got two out of three tanks, a fairly large-scale but still unsuccessful infantry attack took place. Lt-Col R. S. Burton, who then commanded 1st Battery, continues the

story in the *RA Commemoration Book*:
'The next attempt the Italians made to break through was during the night, again on the seaward side of the road. Lt K. Pinnington (afterwards killed in Greece) did extremely well with the guns he commanded and knocked out many vehicles and guns at extremely close range. The Italian attempt to break through was foolishly carried out; they appeared to be completely unable to avoid the herd instinct and large groups of bunched vehicles afforded good targets in the moonlight. A small party of tanks and vehicles succeeded in breaking through down the main road. For some reason the company commander had lifted the mines that he had laid down on the road the night before.

'One of the Bofors covering the road got a shell through the shield, which killed the layer and wounded the rest of the detachment. The gun itself was removed and found serviceable and did good work in the dawn battle later.

'At daybreak the Italians attempted their last breakthrough and were only stopped when right in our position. Lt Kernan of the 2nd Anti-tank Battery had arrived with two more Bofors so that we had eleven in action by this time. All our anti-tank guns did very well. Two tanks were knocked out a few yards from 2nd Rifle Brigade's Battalion HQ and a number were now burning fiercely on the main road. Two of the anti-tank guns put up a gallant fight there before being knocked out at a range of a very few yards by the tanks — but these were all dealt with by other guns soon after. C Battery, 4th RHA, brought accurate and rapid fire down close in front of our position. Sergeant Gould, of 106th RHA, knocked out six tanks at extremely close range with his Bofors on portée — he handled it very cleverly, getting some of the tanks in the rear as they ran down the road past his position. He received an immediate DCM. The battle was soon over and literally thousands of Italian prisoners were taken. They must have been astonished when they realised what a tiny force had prevented their escape to Tripoli.

'Besides these thousands of

prisoners, a tremendous number of guns and vehicles fell into our hands — in fact, this proved to be the end of the Italian army so far as General Wavell's successful campaign was concerned.'

A fortnight before Beda Fomm a Gunner general, Sir Alan Cunningham, had advanced from Kenya into Italian Somaliland with a force of three divisions, while Lt-Gen Sir William Platt, with two divisions, moved into Eritrea, the other Italian East African colony. Cunningham met little resistance, captured Italian Somaliland (with large dumps of petrol) in a month and in little more than a further month had marched through southern Ethiopia to its capital Addis Ababa.

Platt met more determined resistance in Eritrea, where the fortress of Keren, in a defile between formidable mountains, resisted for over a month. After its fall on 27 March Platt marched quickly south to link with Cunningham 400 miles north of Addis Ababa. Here, on 5 May, they received the surrender of the main Italian army in East Africa.

Another Gunner, Lt-Col Orde Wingate, commanding a force of some 1,500 Sudanese and Ethiopians with British officers and NCOs, escorted the Emperor Haile Selassie back to his native land. Advancing from the west, and opposed by an Italian Colonial formation, he finally took its surrender on 20 May, capturing some 1,100 Italians and 14,500 Colonial troops.

These campaigns deprived the Italians of more than 400,000 soldiers and permanently removed the threat from East Africa. Wavell, however, was now forced to hold Cyrenaica with minimum strength and to build up a British expeditionary force for Greece, now under threat of Axis attack. The Greeks were well able to deal with an Italian offensive through Albania, but in April 1941, when German armies invaded both Greece and Yugoslavia from the north, the British force moved across the Mediterranean. The subsequent fighting in Greece and Crete led to an Allied disaster in which 25,000 British and Australians were lost, together with much equipment.

Meanwhile a fresh German-Italian force had concentrated in Tripolitania under the redoubtable general Erwin Rommel and, on 24 March, moved against the weak and largely inexperienced British and Australian forces on the Cyrenaican frontier. In a fortnight this offensive, in which three British generals were captured, had reached Egypt. Wavell, however, demonstrated his strategic stature by leaving a garrison in the fortress port of Tobruk on the flank of Rommel's communications, relying on British seapower to maintain it.

The 9th Australian Infantry Division formed the initial framework of the Tobruk garrison and its commander, Maj-Gen L. G. Morshead, commanded the fortress. The British 3rd Armoured Brigade held an assortment of armoured cars and tanks. The CRA

East African Campaign 1941

51
Lt-Gen Sir Alan Cunningham. *IWM*

52
The Emperor of Abyssinia with (left) Maj (later Lt-Col) O. C. Wingate. *IWM*

51

52

(Commander, Royal Artillery) was Brig L. F. Thompson and he controlled four regiments of 18pdr or 25pdr field guns and two of 37mm or 2pdr anti-tank guns. Brig J. N. Slater commanded the 4th AA brigade which included slightly more than a regiment of 3.7in HAA guns and slightly more than two regiments of Bofors LAA guns.

The Italian defences of Tobruk had included an anti-tank ditch and this was used as the basis of the outer perimeter defences. It was not, for the most part, an effective obstacle, nor were there sufficient mines to make a formidable minefield. It had to be accepted that the enemy would penetrate the defences; when they did, as the British Official History puts it, 'they must then be made to regret it'. This is where the Gunners came in.

The positions were occupied on 9 and 10 April; on the 11th the Germans made a strong fighting reconnaissance with tanks and infantry. Our artillery reacted strongly and, in one battery at least, ammunition ran short. BSM (now Lt-Col) A. J. Batten, then of A/E Battery, 1st RHA, has a story from that day's events which illustrates the sometimes strained relations between the soldier at the sharp end of a battle and the 'base-wallah' clinging to routine. As ammunition ran short, Batten sent a lorry back for a load, the

driver however being turned away from the dump as he had no indent. Batten then sent a bombardier with the lorry, instructing him to explain the situation and, if no ammunition was forthcoming, to help himself. He lent the bombardier his pistol.

Soon after dusk on the 13th, Easter Day, Rommel began his first serious assault on Tobruk with an attempt to establish a bridgehead over the tank ditch, west of the El Adem road. An Australian Battalion bore the brunt of

this attack and repulsed it. It was renewed in the small hours, however, and by dawn a small bridgehead had been achieved, through which the tanks passed, heading north. The Australians stayed-put and did great execution among the German infantry.

The German tanks moved forward in the half-light, engaged from the flank by 2pdrs of M Battery, 3rd RHA. Eventually they came upon A and E Troops of 1st RHA with their 25pdrs.

Here, from the Royal Artillery Commemoration Book, is the story of one of A Troop's subalterns who, relieved at an Australian Company HQ an hour before dawn, made his way back to his guns to the sound of tank movement behind him.
'Peter Hemans, commanding A/E Battery, ordered "Tank Alert", but although we could hear the rumbling of tanks it seemed an age before anything happened. At last six black objects huddled together in groups of three appeared to the right front of the Troop. It was still very dark and difficult to judge the range, but we set our sights at 400 and opened fire.

'The first shot from No 1 gun set the leading tank on fire. No 2's first round lifted the turret clean off another tank — a good start, but we had stirred up a hornets' nest. Soon there were 15 or more tanks firing at us with 75mms and machine guns. We scored hit after hit, but I fancy we put a number of shells into tanks that were already dead. During this period two officers — the only officers with the guns — and four other ranks were hit. The tanks were now working round our right towards E Troop. Just as our No. 1 gun swung round to engage them, a 75-mm shell landed on the trail, killing all the detachment and setting fire to a box of cartridges. At the same time a gun of E Troop received a direct hit on the shield, disabling the whole detachment. The Battery Segeant-Major (Batten), although wounded, manned the gun himself and continued to fire.

Nos 2, 3 and 4 guns were in great heart, and every time a tank was hit a cheer went up. For perhaps half an hour the battle continued thus; then gradually the firing slackened till all was quiet. The surviving tanks had pulled back.'

These surviving tanks turned eastwards but ran into the guns of the Australian anti-tank regiment and of British tanks in hull-down positions. Sixteen of their 38 tanks eventually recrossed the ditch, their withdrawal and that of the infantry being well harassed.

A further attempt, upon the western

April to October 1941, over 4,000 aircraft were engaged by the AA gunners of Tobruk, between three and four hundred being damaged or destroyed, for an expenditure of some 150,000 rounds of ammunition and 170 casualties.

The Axis forces in North Africa could be sustained only from Italy and between Italy and those forces lay the small island of Malta, a vital base for British sea and air power. The vulnerability of Malta was always obvious and plans for her reinforcement were made in 1939; from many causes they could not be fully implemented. Even when fighter aircraft and AA guns were available in fair quantity, the air defence of the island had to overcome many problems — a lack of outlying warning posts and mutual interference of aircraft and AA guns being two of the principal ones, whilst the running through of convoys to Malta was always hazardous.

The prospect of invasion, which at first seemed high, led to the provision of beach defences while the 'Grand Harbour', at Valetta on the north coast, was well provided with Coast Artillery.

sector, was discontinued three days later and Tobruk was not to suffer another serious landward attack before its relief. Rommel established himself on the Egyptian frontier and beat off two efforts to dislodge him. Tobruk he left to the Luftwaffe, which made continued and determined attacks on the harbour and the shipping on which the garrison depended for its survival. In the eight months from

On 26 July 1941 the Italians, using small surface craft, made an attempt to penetrate the harbour defences and destroy shipping therein, this leading to one of the few coast artillery actions of the war and to the sole operational use of the '6pdr Twin'.

The assault force consisted of the *Diana*, a fast 'E-boat carrier', two large motor torpedo boats (MAS), two midget submarines with detachable explosive bows (universally described as 'Pigs'), a carrier for the Pigs (MTL), a flotilla leader (MTS) with nine midget motor torpedo boats with fixed torpedo bows (MT) and, not least, a very brave team of 36 men. The *Diana* unloaded her craft at about 1.30am some four miles north of the harbour entrance; she had produced an 'echo' in an RAF early-warning radar, and this helped to alert the defence. An Italian air raid had been arranged as a diversion but on far too small scale to be effective — it took place at 4.15am by which time the Pigs, followed by the nine MT, were on their way to the first objective, the viaduct of the outer mole, which carried an anti-submarine net below it.

Both Pigs maintained their reputation and disappeared, one being surrendered later. This left the field to the MT, the leader of which directed his craft at the viaduct, baled out but was disappointed at the lack of subsequent explosion. The pilot of the second MT stayed aboard, drove into the viaduct and died when the two MTs exploded together, bringing down the outer span of the viaduct but failing to open a route into the harbour; it was now about 4.45am. The wake of the second craft had been spotted by a look-out of the St Elmo 6pdr Twin battery, who gave the alarm. Four further white waves followed the first. Col H. A. R. Ferro, Royal Malta Artillery, was the battery commander. The following excerpts are from his account, as recorded in the *Royal Artillery Journal* of March 1972:

'Twelve seconds after opening fire Lance-Bombardier Bugeja, having corrected twice and bracketed his target, hit it. It blew up under a twenty-foot column of spray. The enemy formation began to break, but two seconds later Sergeant Zammit on ''G'' gun hit his target, followed in two more seconds by Sergeant Barbara on ''F'' gun hitting his.'

Two of the pilots now baled out and 'Cease firing' was ordered, with a view to recovering the MTs. Neighbouring searchlights, however, illuminated

60

61

Maritime Royal Artillery

Formed in 1941 to provide guns and detachments for the defence of merchant vessels

62
Manning Bofors aboard Dutch transport *Dempe* in a North African port. *IWM*

63
Ohio at Malta August 1942. Severe submarine and air attacks were made on this tanker and her convoy. *Ohio* was immobilised, abandoned, reboarded and towed into Malta. Of 161 Maritime gunners in the convoy, 28 were killed and 11 (including Bombardier Labern of *Ohio's* detachment) were awarded the Naval Distinguished Service Medal. *IWM*

OPs in the Desert

Observation Posts were an essential to effective gunnery. The desert, however, was often flat and it required ingenuity to find OPs.

64
A hole, in ground which is slightly above the surrounding level, in this case overlooking Tobruk during the advance of January 1941. *IWM*

65
Lysander army-cooperation aircraft. RAF pilots observed and reported fall-of-shot in the January and February (1941) operations for Bardia and Tobruk. Procedures were slow, however, and aircraft vulnerable. Fighter cover was needed. Artillery observation of this kind was discontinued, and Gunners had to wait almost two years for its renewal. *IWM*

66
A house in Derna. *IWM*

67
The height of impudence. Lt A. H. P. Carr and Sgt D. J. Lamb of 107 RHA (South Notts Hussars), FOOs in the Tobruk siege.
Australian War Memorial Neg No 20383

three craft some three miles outside the harbour — probably the MTL, MTS and lost MT. They were engaged by 6in guns, the MTL being hit, immobilised and finally sunk by Hurricane aircraft.

An hour later, the MT leader having been recovered from the harbour and made prisoner, the two other pilots that had baled out suddenly reboarded their craft, started the engines and set out towards the north. They were engaged by seven 6pdrs from two different batteries, by Bofors LAA guns in three different positions and by infantry machine guns, providing a notable firework display which was watched by large crowds on the waterfront. Sgt Barbara's gun hit one of the MTs; the other pilot again baled out but did not survive the explosion as his craft was hit.

Soon afterwards Ferro's attention

was called to an MAS visible in outline in the light of dawn. Ferro continues:

'Its range, taken on the Depression Range Finder, was 6,000 yards. The maximum range of the 6-pdr gun was 5,500 yards. We decided to test the accuracy of that figure. One round was fired. The shell landed short and, so far as we could estimate, it was just about 500 yards short. What we did not know at the time, was that the shell had ricochetted off the water, and by a chance in a million, had bounced about 500 yards, to the cabin of the ''MAS''. It exploded inside, killing Capitano Moccagatta and the crew of ''MAS No. 452''.'

Of the Italian assault force, only the *Diana*, with one MT, escaped.

In Egypt, in the autumn of 1941, Gen Sir Claude Auchinleck, who had relieved Gen Wavell in July, was completing his plans for a November offensive. The Eighth Army had now been formed, commanded by Gen Sir Alan Cunningham and containing XIII and XXX Corps. The plan was for XXX Corps to pass round Rommel's southern flank and thrust northwards to the higher ground about Sidi Rezegh, some 18 miles south-west of Tobruk. XIII Corps would attack westwards from the Egyptian frontier, and the Tobruk garrison would break-out upon the enemy's left flank and rear.

On 18 November XXX Corps's advance began and on the following day 7th Armoured Brigade seized the Sidi Rezegh ridge and airfield. This was occupied by 7th Armoured Division's 'Support Group', principally composed of the division's artillery and infantry and commanded by the CRA of the division, Brig Jock Campbell. On the 21st the 'sortie' from Tobruk was due and Campbell was placed in command of the attack northwards from Sidi Rezegh to link up with it. In his Group were the 1st King's Royal Rifle Corps, the 2nd Rifle Brigade, 3rd RHA (2pdr anti-tank guns), 60th Field Regiment with a battery of 51st Field Regiment (25pdrs) and 2nd LAA Battery (40mm Bofors guns). In support was 6th Royal Tank Regiment.

In the event a strong force of German armour and infantry attacked

from the north; 7th Division's Support Group found itself fighting a savage two-day defensive battle and here Jock Campbell won the Victoria Cross.

Another of the four VCs of this battle was won by 2-Lt George Ward Gunn of J Battery, 3rd RHA. His Troop of four 2pdr anti-tank guns was one of three in support of the Rifle Brigade. They were attacked by 60 tanks and, while disabling many of these, one gun after another was knocked-out until there survived only one, standing on a burning portée with its detachment dead beside it. Ward Gunn and his battery commander Maj Bernard Pinney ran to the portée and, while the latter fought the fire, Ward Gunn manned the gun. Two more tanks were destroyed and others probably damaged before the fire of the remainder was concentrated on the one gun, Ward Gunn being killed. Pinney survived, only to be killed on the following day.

For some the most graphic picture of this chaotic Sidi Rezegh battle may be obtained from the following extracts of an account by Gnr Geoffrey Bennett, who started the battle as a 2pdr portée-driver in D Battery, transferred to gun layer in the course of it, and ended up as acting, unpaid No 1.

After a night spent largely in constructing a 2pdr gunpit out of hard rock, his troop moved forward on to the airfield and prepared to breakfast. 'The "biscuit burgoo" (boiled biscuits), our usual breakfast, was almost ready when our "old man" drove up. Major W. B. Stewart, O.C. "D" Battery, RHA, was an officer of the Pinney mould. Incredible courage, remarkable bravery he was to show in the days ahead. "Support Group (infantry and artillery) are to attack at 0830 hours, and you, B Troop, are to support a company of KRRC" (or RB, I forget which). We reported to Major Chance, company commander. So much for the "burgoo" and an army and its stomach.

'Five German Mark III and IV tanks opened up at us, as we crossed the machine-gun-fire infested airfield. We were absolutely no match. A hull-down position, five 50-mm and 75-mm guns and machine-guns against two 2-prs, conspicuous and unprotected. The bren-gunner decapitated, driver mortally wounded and loader slightly hit, I was sent back, on foot of course across that fire-swept airfield, for help.

69

A ''B'' Troop replacement arrived, dead buried (with difficulty), one wounded (my best friend) almost dead, transferred to RAMC, caught up, and the attack — one of the finest infantry actions of the war — successful.

'General Gott and the Brigadier (Campbell) both standing there. ''Believe that the fifty-odd tanks you see out there are out of petrol, but we'll attack them when replenished. The Brigadier orders that there will be no withdrawals: Last man! Last round!'', said the officer. And so it was.'

Gunner Bennett then described how a 'mainly artillery battle' developed, of a ferocity and intensity beyond comprehension, in which were involved the 3rd and 4th Regiments, RHA, 60th Field Regiment, 1st LAA Regiment and 107th Regiment, RHA (The Northumberland Hussars).
' ''Gun Control!''
'The Brigadier and Major Stewart dashing from gun to gun, 25s, 2-pdrs, urging, praising, encouraging, directing fire; dragging bodies out of their way, they took their place. Bombed, shelled, mortared, machine-gunned and ''tanked'', the British gunners stood their ground. Swirling dust: confusion: noise. Portées lurching forward, horns blowing; crews brutally battered to death — on fire. Prisoners on both sides taken and retaken. Casualty clearing stations completely annihilated, and reminiscent of slaughterhouses. Fires everywhere, exploding ammunition, the sweet sickly smell of blood ... Brigadier Campbell, that fanatically

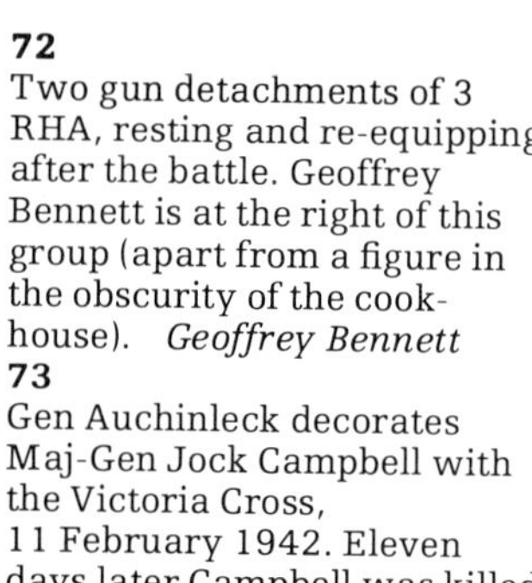

72
Two gun detachments of 3 RHA, resting and re-equipping after the battle. Geoffrey Bennett is at the right of this group (apart from a figure in the obscurity of the cook-house). *Geoffrey Bennett*

73
Gen Auchinleck decorates Maj-Gen Jock Campbell with the Victoria Cross, 11 February 1942. Eleven days later Campbell was killed in a car accident in the desert. *IWM*

brave, absolutely flawless, loved and idolised soldier by men of the Western Desert, was cheered by his troops as, blue flag held high, he led in an armoured brigade. Our sergeant, saluting, ordered ''Follow the Brigadier''. ''No'', Jock shouted, and indicated with the palm of his hand. After a lull, which brought last light, our wounded taken away, mortars opened up with a ferocity indicating an infantry attack. We were leaving the wadi when I (that is the portée) received a direct hit, badly wounding the No. 1 in the face.

'I can't remember what happened during the night, apart from remembering the No. 1's courage and our plying him with chianti — captured in the attack. We learned that ''D'' HQ had been captured almost intact, but our LAD came and hooked me up for a suspended tow.'

They were towed to the 'B Echelon' area for repair or replacement.
'Suddenly this massive B Echelon area ''took-off'', and thousands (there must have been) of soft-skinned vehicles — with pedals down, in hopeless panic — sped, they knew not where, in total disorder, across the blue. Panzers firing a few rounds into the mass did not help. The amazing Brigadier eventually sorted order out of absolute chaos, and gained control . . .

'I left the wounded at an ADS which was hurriedly being assembled. The MO told me to get my desert sores dressed before I left, but when I heard the screams of a soldier having a leg

amputation without anaesthetic — so I was told — I left, not unemotionally.'

With his gun and a repaired portée, Gunner Bennett set out in the direction of the noise of battle and met his Regimental CO, Lt-Col Wilson, apparently acting as CRA. He told Bennett to report to the Northumberland Hussars, where he would be the No 1 of the gun and where his detachment would be made up to strength.
'Reporting as detailed, I got a Rhodesian gunner and a J Battery driver and was told to line up with the rest — just in time for the last grand shambles that was the Sidi Rezegh battle. Withdrawing in face of this ferocious attack — fire everywhere — at last light, the troop commander came alongside, told me to bring up the rear, and to travel on a bearing of 180 degrees for eight miles.

'The column moved off in an orderly fashion, although pursued. We'd just begun to move when the engine gave a couple of last gasps and the vehicle stopped — and not in ideal conditions to trace the fault. No navigational aids, but with more than a little desert lore and experience (pouring petrol direct into the carburettor), I reported to my new troop commander a few hours late. ''I'd given you up'', he said, and congratulated us on a marvellous show after hearing all about it.

'Their tiffies worked all night with inspection lamps and ground sheets all round the vehicle — to no avail. At first light the TC sent for me and said,

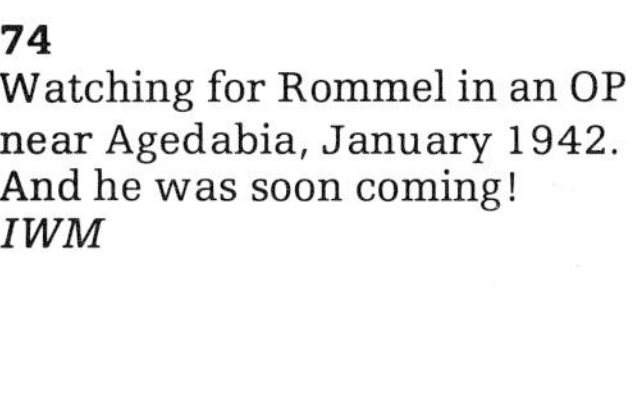

Watching for Rommel in an OP near Agedabia, January 1942. And he was soon coming! *IWM*

''Sorry, you've put up a wonderful show, but you are no use to me if you can't fight''. He told me where he thought the enemy was and they moved off. Unattached; three men and a damaged vehicle, a good gun and not a soul in sight.'

They were taken unwillingly on tow by an armoured car of the 11th Hussars and then by some South Africans, finally reaching the Corps Workshop and a ration-issue. And, some days later, back to D Battery.

At this stage in the battle Auchinleck came forward to consult Cunningham who, concerned at the enemy's tank superiority, thought that Auchinleck should seriously consider withdrawal to the Egyptian frontier. Auchinleck declined to do so and, returning to his headquarters, replaced Cunningham by Gen Neil Ritchie from his own staff.

Rommel meanwhile took the unexpected step of launching his two Panzer divisions due east towards Egypt, scything their way through XXX Corps's supply and maintenance areas and causing chaos and widespread break-down of communications. The panzers, however, struck stern resistance from XIII Corps, were soon in considerable embarrassment for lack of tank fuel and ammunition and on 26 November were recalled.

Auchinleck is generally given credit for standing fast and Cunningham blamed for recommending withdrawal, but the picture is in fact less clear. Rommel's dash for Egypt is thought by some to have been foolhardly and to have led directly to the necessity for his subsequent withdrawal from Cyrenaica; had he, as expected, moved his Panzer Divisions against XXX Corps south of Sidi Rezegh, Cunningham's recommendation could have proved correct, though by then, perhaps, too late.

Sidi Rezegh was to change hands thrice more before Tobruk was relieved on 9 December. More tank (and gun versus tank) engagements took place as Rommel withdrew, in good order, to El Agheila on the Gulf of Sydra.

Desert tactics, during the past 12 months, had developed into a form much divorced from the well-understood tactics of prewar days. In some ways it more resembled naval than conventional army tactics. Armoured formations moved across featureless wastes, trying to intercept weaker bodies of the enemy. The function of the unarmoured infantry and artillery was to hold ground wherein their armour could 'laager' by night or against which the enemy armour might immolate itself. In the latter role, defended areas were often described as 'boxes'. Artillery, with infantry or less frequently armour, was also organised into small 'columns' to obtain information or raid enemy supplies. Often, therefore, the gun detachments found themselves in action in the open, without time to dig-in, unarmoured, against enemy tanks.

This was all very well in the early

75
Knightsbridge. *IWM*

days, to harass the Italians with their lightly armed and armoured tanks; with the appearance of the German tanks it became a different matter. The 2pdr gun packed too small a punch to deal with these, except at the shortest ranges. The 25pdr, designed to kill infantry, was used more and more in the anti-tank role. Its detachments fought with the greatest gallantry but the harm they could do was limited, while the German tanks could stand off in hull-down positions and destroy the guns with long-range fire. For fire-power to be effective it needed to be concentrated but this was not easy to achieve within the dashing but dispersed manoeuvres of this era.

An article by 'MD', published in the *Royal Artillery Journal* during 1944, gives a revealing picture of a Gunner's life in a 'Desert Column'. The writer commanded 370th Battery of 51st Field Regiment which, late in 1941, formed a column with the Coldstream Guards and a 2pdr anti-tank troop. On their first day out, the writer was detached with a troop of 25pdrs and three 2pdrs to form a 'strongpoint' (surely an over-statement), where nothing was done but a little harassing fire 'while the battle of Sidi Rezegh raged to the north-east'.

On the next day they learnt that the enemy was behind them and were told to withdraw and rejoin the main column. Compass was used to maintain direction and vehicle-speedometers to estimate distance.

At dawn next morning their observation posts reported tanks approaching. These were shelled at long range and down to 5,000 yards; the guns then waited to engage at short-range but their target turned out to be one of their own regiments. And, of the following night, the battery commander wrote: 'I withdrew the OPs to the gun area and after dark wireless communication with Regimental Headquarters failed, and we went to bed, a solitary battery in the desert wondering where the enemy tanks were.'

Eventually, describing how four of his guns were overrun by tanks which appeared at close range out of a mist, he commented: 'This was one of many small columns and boxes mopped up by the enemy, and feeling grew that columns were not a good thing now that Germans were in the desert with big tanks.'

On 7 December 1941 Japan had joined the Axis powers; although this brought the United States into the war on the British side, the Eighth Army could expect little in the way of reinforcement until the urgent needs of British Far East garrisons had been met; it badly needed a period to rest and refit. Rommel gave it just a fortnight, before advancing once again to the attack on 21 January 1942; the forward defences were quickly overrun and on the 28th Benghazi fell. Early in February, however, the British succeeded in establishing a line of defended 'boxes' between Gazala in the north and Bir Hacheim, 60 miles to the south, where the 'Free French' held the flank position. Behind this line of 'boxes', and sustained by others in the rear, was the bulk of the British armour.

The most famous of the British 'boxes' was 'Knightsbridge', a small plateau in the desert containing a shallow depression about 600 yards square and little else to distinguish it but a notice-board proclaiming its identity and, helpfully, its map reference. It lay at the intersection of two of the principal desert tracks and its formidable garrison included the 2nd Regiment RHA, with 25pdrs, C Battery of 102nd Anti-tank Regiment (Northumberland Hussars), with newly-issued 6pdr anti-tank guns, and two troops of 43rd LAA Regiment, with Bofors 40mms. Guns and vehicles were thoroughly dug-in, to the extent that

76
The end of an enemy tank.
IWM

77
Quad, with 25pdr, moving
through a dust storm. *IWM*

vehicles' roofs were below ground level.

On 27 May Rommel rounded Bir Hacheim and appeared opposite Knightsbridge. Several infantry attacks were made from the south, supported by artillery but, with relatively good observation, the British artillery regularly repelled them. Tank attacks followed and the new 6pdrs were used to some effect. After this, apart from occasional dive-bombing, attacks on the Knightsbridge 'box' were discontinued.

West-south-west and some five miles from Knightsbridge was a depression in the desert, some four miles by two in area, into which Rommel's armour moved and to which the title 'Cauldron' was given. To the west was the original British minefield and beyond it the main concentration of German infantry and artillery. The German engineers made gaps through the minefield to establish communication with Rommel, who thus refuelled and refitted his units east of the minefield. Gen Ritchie decided to capture the Cauldron; his plan was for the 10th Indian Infantry Brigade to penetrate the enemy's anti-tank screen by a night attack, 22nd Armoured Brigade then passing through to the west of the Cauldron and leaving the bulk of 7th Armoured Division and 9th Indian Infantry Brigade to destroy the enemy within it. The first phase of the attack was to be supported by a very heavy artillery concentration.

On the night of 4/5 June the first objectives in the Cauldron were captured at trifling cost, but the main enemy positions proved to be further west than had been thought and escaped the main weight of the British artillery fire. 22nd Armoured Brigade, supported by 25pdrs of 107th Regiment, RHA (The South Notts Hussars) and 6pdrs of the Northumberland Hussars, moved off by moonlight and at dawn were on the western lip of the Cauldron, where they came under heavy fire. This our guns suppressed and 22nd Brigade's tanks went through to engage enemy armour further west. The South Notts OPs, meanwhile, had magnificent observation into the Cauldron, which was thick with enemy, and did great execution. The 2nd Highland Light Infantry, however, who had followed the tanks into the Cauldron, were decimated by casualties and were withdrawn. The 3rd/9th Jat Regiment (from 9th Indian Infantry Brigade) came to the support of the 2nd/4th Gurkha Rifles in the north-east corner of the Cauldron, where also was 28th Field Regiment. South of the Cauldron 4th Field Regiment supported the 4th/10th Baluchis and 157th Field Regiment, in general support of 10th Brigade, were in action west of 4th Regiment. The headquarters of 10th Brigade and 7th Armoured Division were at Bir Harmat, five miles south of Knightsbridge and south-east of the Cauldron.

Maj K. M. Goddard, then Intelligence Officer of 28th Field Regiment, describes in a *Gunner Magazine* article his visit, with his CO, to a Divisional briefing on 5 June:
'That afternoon I accompanied Col. Needham to a Divisional briefing close to Bir Harmat (5 miles south of Knightsbridge) where Brigade and Divisional headquarters were now located very near our starting point. Here we found the remnants of 2HLI, who had been withdrawn, resting and nearby was a battalion of the DCLI just arrived from Iran. In the midst of the briefing an attack developed SW of Bir Harmat and the whole area was swept by heavy machine gun fire. There was no armour or artillery to defend the position and we later learned that the DCLI had been completely overrun. The CO and I made a hasty departure northwards and when out of range we stopped and looking back saw all the soft skinned vehicles of command and B Echelon groups streaming eastwards. We turned to the West and, soon after, rejoined our batteries which had now moved up to the northern lip of the Cauldron and were facing South.'

In the evening 22nd Armoured Brigade withdrew to refuel and refit, intending to return to the fray at dawn on the 6th. In the now chaotic conditions east of the battlefield they seem to have had difficulty in locating their maintenance echelons and did not return. Nor was there now any effective higher control, on the British side, of the battle in and around the Cauldron where was played out, in the words of the *Official British War History* (HMSO), 'a splendid and tragic episode in the history of the Royal Artillery, for the Gunners fought their guns to the last and died where they stood.'

During the night the guns were emplaced as well as possible, although all the batteries found themselves on hard rock very difficult to break up. Capt Melvill Milner, then Battery Captain of 4th Battery of 4th Field Regiment, has written as follows:
'Soon after 0700 hours of that fateful morning of the 6th June 1942, enemy 88s started firing at our guns from a hidden position. We only had seven 25-prs at this stage, having lost one through a premature two days before. We soon began to suffer casualties. An order came through to cease fire as we were wasting our ammunition firing at vague targets. We were to wait until the German armour came within our "sure-kill" tank range of the 25-pounder, namely 1500 yards. We lost two guns through direct hits and, shortly after this, the battery commander was hit and he ordered me to

take command. He was evacuated by bren carrier.

'The spearhead of the German attack was now apparent, this being the 15th Panzer Division, led by 60 heavy tanks, which were advancing very slowly towards us. When I judged that the leader-panzers were about 1500 yards away, I gave the order "Gun Control" which meant that each one of the remaining five gun commanders would pick his own targets and give his own orders to fire. The slow advance of the panzers was fantastic. It seemed as though the entire Afrika Korps was coming towards us.

'By now our regimental aid post, a slight dip in the ground with a vehicle or two, was a place of much suffering and our medical officer, Captain D. B. Watson, RAMC, was struggling with an impossible task: no one man can deal with the ever-increasing number of casualties being suffered by a regiment in the process of destruction. All we could do was to collect more wounded and collect field-dressings from our dead.

'We were still under fire from the hidden 88's, which were picking our guns off from our right to left. The panzers did not appear to be firing at us at this stage but when they came closer it became a fight between gunners in tanks and gunners in the open — flesh against steel. An 88-mm shell hit the ground in front of my batman-driver and failed to explode, rolling between us. Tucker and I looked at each other and then breathed again. Our RHQ, near the RAP, was a hole in the ground covered by a tarpaulin. It was a salubrious dwelling-place compared with our gun position and battery headquarters, which were fully exposed. Getting the wounded away from the guns became more difficult as the tank-versus-gun battle warmed up and then came the moment when our last gun was knocked out.

'The gun position was now a dreadful place, with smashed guns, dead, wounded and burnt-out vehicles all over the place. We had inflicted much damage on the Germans but they had destroyed us.

'The panzers now advanced across the Baluchi position and we could see the infantry being "winkled" out of their trenches. It was all over: men in the open without anti-tank guns cannot fight tanks, however great their hearts.'

This battle was over by mid-morning; the story of 28th Field Regiment on the north side of the Cauldron and that of 167th Regiment to the south-east were very similar. To the west, with 22nd Brigade's reconnaissance regiment the Royal Northumberland Fusiliers, were the 25pdrs of the South Notts Hussars and the 6pdrs of the Northumberland Hussars; this whole group, under Lt-Col E. P. A. des Graz of the Fusiliers, was still in action. The following extracts from an account in the *Royal Artillery Commemoration Book*, prepared from survivors' reports, tell their story. Col Seely, mentioned therein, was CO of the South Notts Hussars:

'Suddenly at 8.30am the enemy fire was concentrated on Birkin's battery (425th), then on to the Baluchis battery German tanks moved in, making for E Troop of 425th, and a brisk and deadly exchange took place. Then, as the dust and smoke cleared away the enemy withdrew, leaving ten tanks behind, knocked out a few hundred yards from the guns of 425th Battery. The gunners were delighted and settled down to await the next attack. It was not long in coming. The enemy moved further west, to attack the units on 425th's left flank. A few minutes of intense small arms and machine-gun fire — then dead silence. The position had been overrun. A handful of men were seen staggering off under heavy escort. This left 425th Battery with an exposed flank, and a hasty rearrangement had to be made. But a little later Stukas flew over the position and the ring of purple sent up by the enemy to show his forward positions to the planes made it clear that the box was now completely surrounded.

'Never for a moment did the shelling stop. Casualties became heavier and heavier. Vehicles were burning everywhere. The enemy with their guns just out of sight could direct their fire with great accuracy on the mass of men and vehicles and guns in the Cauldron below. Captain Bennett, hit through the leg, arrived at the Command Post to report his troop position untenable. Three of his gun detachments had been knocked out, but the guns themselves were intact. BSM Hardy and a driver were immediatly despatched in a quad to pull the guns in 400 yards, a feat which they accomplished most gallantly in spite of heavy machine-gun fire.

'The next attack came in very quickly and soon German tanks had overrun the infantry battalion in the rear and were nosing about amongst the burning vehicles round the Bir. Captain Trippier and his Northumberland Hussars were quite magnificent. Under heavy fire they man-handled their anti-tank guns across to try to safeguard our rear, but they were all knocked out. He then drove back with his truck full of badly wounded men to report that he had not a man left. As he spoke a shell exploding beside him wounded him severely. Events moved quickly now and amazing things happened as the fighting raged at close quarters. A sergeant of the Recce Regiment with what was left of his section leaped on a German tank, trying to ram hand grenades through the turret. They were killed to a man. The machine-gun fire was intense. Cartridge boxes went up in a sheet of flame. Four lorry loads of Germans in British 3-tonners drove straight past the guns untouched. A staff car and two generals drove to the Command Post and, as the gunners jumped at it, accelerated and got away. The doctor and his orderly worked unceasingly in a murderous fire round the Command Post, which was a shambles of dead and wounded. As the gun detachments were killed signallers, drivers and Northumberland ''Geordies'' crawled over to take their places.

'Colonel Seely, who had been constantly on the move around his Regiment in his Honey tank, encouraging the men by his splendid example, arrived at 426th Battery Command Post during the early afternoon and suddenly observed three German infantry lorries appearing over the escarpment about 1,000 yards north of F Troop. The German infantry jumped out, but before they could get into action with their light automatics they were met by the concentrated fire of F Troop, the 6-pdr anti-tank guns of the Northumberland Hussars and the small arms of the Recce Regiment. In a few moments the lorries were in flames and the scattered German survivors rounded up.

'About 3pm the Germans were attacking the right of the position. Of the anti-tank guns one only now remained, but there was no one to man it until a young lance-bombardier, with one arm blown off at the elbow, crawled out in a vain attempt to reach it. Colonel des Graz walked over from his blazing and useless vehicle, but was killed immediately as he tried to fire

the anti-tank gun. Communication still remained. For 16 hours the signal sergeant had sat in his vehicle keeping on the air to Brigade. The second-in-command spoke to the Brigadier and told him that if he would get some ammunition through with some tanks, we could hold out until dark. The Brigadier wished him luck, but at that moment the vehicle was hit and up it went.

'As evening approached, everywhere the German tanks were moving in. The Indian Infantry Brigade was completely overrun — there was nothing left. Nearly every vehicle was burning and heavy smoke obliterated the sky. Still the South Notts Hussars held out and kept the tanks at bay. Guns were facing every direction — wherever a tank could be seen working up through the smoke. Solid shot tore up the ground all round. As a last desperate measure it was decided to move the guns of Captain's Pringle's E Troop to the rear, despite the enemy's immediate reaction to any sign of movement.

'The quads drove up and the men — all that were left of them — leapt to hook in the guns. But before they had gone 200 yards all four of the quads went up in flames. Major Birkin, hurrying to see what could be done, had his armoured car hit by an AP shot and his invaluable BSM, Hardy, killed beside him. By the time he had regained his remaining A Troop, of which only two guns were still in action, the enemy tanks were on top of the position and the gallant fight of 425th Battery was over.

'Down in the hollow, Alan Chadburn's guns were still intact, but on all sides the German tanks were closing in, machine guns blazing. Colonel Seely and Bish Peal, his adjutant, who had continued to ply indomitably about the battlefield, had their tank hit and set on fire. Both died later in enemy hands. The end was very near now. 426th Battery Command Post fell to the advancing tanks; and though in a last defiant gesture Chadburn's F Troop scored two direct hits at 800 yards they could do no more. The groups of British prisoners appearing over the escarpment put further firing out of the question, and the survivors of 426th Battery turned sadly to their final task — the battering of their gun sights. For a few moments more the air sang with machine-gun bullets; then all was quiet, and that deep silence that

Retreat to El Alamein

78
25pdr of 2 (Indian) Field Regiment coming into action in support of 3rd Indian Motor Brigade. *IWM*

79
6pdr gun on portée, 4 (Rhodesian) Anti-tank Battery. *IWM*

rison into Tobruk. The withdrawal took place without major disaster but this time Rommel made no mistake with Tobruk, striking on the 20th before any adequate defence was ready and capturing the fortress and 30,000 prisoners.

Auchinleck, assuming personal control of the battle, selected a defensive line 65 miles west of Alexandria, between El Alamein on the Mediterranean coast and the northern edge of the Qattara Depression, an area of saltpan and quicksands impassable to vehicles. Into these defences the Eighth Army withdrew and before them the Axis forces appeared at the end of what was now a very long and difficult supply line.

On 1 July 1942 Rommel made his first move against the El Alamein position and by nightfall had made inroads which threatened an important feature of the position, the Ruweisat ridge. A makeshift force, 'Robcol', under the Gunner Brig R. P. Waller, was hastily posted on the ridge, its principal components being 11th Field Regiment and the 1st/4th Essex. During 2 July the position was gradually reinforced but, before this had borne fruit, the original force needed to fight a desperate battle. Great valour was displayed, none perhaps exceeding that of Lance-Bombardier J. R. Johnson who lost an arm early in the morning, but continued through the day to lay and fire his gun — to die in hospital on the 3rd. On the evening of the 2nd the enemy withdrew from the ridge and the Alamein position was gradually stabilised.

A year previously Winston Churchill had, with the concurrence of his military advisers, issued a paper to various high commanders on the uses of artillery and air support. The paper opened with the arresting sentence, 'Renown awaits the Commander who first in this war restores Artillery to its prime importance on the battlefield.'

Churchill, like many others, was thinking primarily of the role of the gun against the tank but, as events were to show, artillery's importance on the battlefield needed to reach, and would indeed reach, into wider spheres than that. Signs had appeared during the 1942 campaigns of some awareness of the need to concentrate artillery fire for worthwhile results, but perhaps the most important seeds had already been sown, in Britain, and were very shortly to flower.

descends on a battlefield when the contest is over spread over the Cauldron.'

Rommel now concentrated on Bir Hacheim at the south end of the defences. By 10 June, lack of ammunition and water brought a gallant French defence to an end. Rommel still could not capture the Knightsbridge 'box' but the British armour could not move him from its perimeter. Ritchie decided to withdraw to the Egyptian frontier but to put a South African gar-

5 Restoration

There were four principal fields of development which combined to restore the artillery to its prime importance on the battlefield, Radar, anti-tank guns, the introduction of self-propelled guns and spectacular trends in the field of Gunnery.

Radar was the name ultimately given to the devices by which radio waves, projected towards enemy aerial or other vehicles and reflected therefrom, could thereafter be examined and deductions made as to the position, direction and speed of movement of the enemy vehicles. Sir Robert Watson-Watt, a British Government research scientist, must be allotted the principal credit for British service developments in the 1930s, concurrently with similar developments in other countries.

At first Radar was used primarily to obtain early warning of enemy aircraft approaching the coast. This was invaluable for the RAF and useful for the AA defences. Between 1940 and 1944, however, Radar sets of greater precision were developed which could be used to give the accurate location of an aircraft, in terms which a modern predictor could use in transmitting continuous data to the guns and, eventually, to apply these automatically. This achieved an enormous improvement in the accuracy of heavy anti-aircraft guns.

Sgt J. R. L. Anderson, RA (later Captain in the 18th Royal Garwhal Rifles) was in 1940 in 285th HAA Battery at Dover. He describes his return from a course towards the end of that year, to find an addition to the establishment in the form of a mysterious hut, out of bounds to all but a team strictly isolated from battery personnel and 'experimenting in methods of fire control'. Anderson's battery did plenty of shooting and this was sometimes controlled from the hut. When under 'hut control' Anderson's predictor and height-finder

detachments did not follow the target visually but instead followed pointers on dials actuated from the hut. Results were sometimes eccentric. Anderson continues:

'Our rather sceptical opinion of the value of the hut was changed radically on a bitter night towards the end of December. It was a horrible night of mist and low cloud, bitterly cold and visibility roughly nil. Searchlights were useless. A big German raid came over and we were manning our guns, but feeling utterly futile. Then we were put on "hut control" and picked up a target, on which we opened fire. On such a night it seemed a waste of ammunition, but after a few rounds there was a tremendous explosion in the sky over the Channel, at what we judged to be the position of our target. It was such a violent explosion that the murk and mist were momentarily torn away and we could see the flash of the explosion through the cloud. We thought that we must have scored an

80
Sir Robert Watson-Watt,
Service Radar pioneer. *IWM*

Radar GL II

For Early-warning and early
experiments in Fire Control.
81
Transmitter. *IWM*
82
Receiver. *IWM*

astonishingly lucky direct hit on the bomb-rack of some German bomber, but in fact what must have happened was that our guns were perfectly directed to the target by this early use of radar. In the small hours of the morning we were stood down and given a rum-ration, which was extraordinarily welcome'.

An important development of Radar was the fitting of miniaturised equipment as a fuze into the warhead of shells, to be activated by the 'echoes' received from the target and thus to burst the shell near it. These fuzes were called 'Variable Time' or VT fuzes and radically increased the destructiveness of HAA fire.

Anti-tank guns and tanks waged a design battle throughout the war in which, until 1944, the Germans had the pull. The British 2pdr had no chance against the German tanks of 1941-42 unless its detachment held their fire down to ranges of 400 yards

83
Early fire-control Radar GL
III, Canadian-built. *IWM*

84
Elsie — the searchlight
Radar. *IWM*

or thereabouts; after that they often needed to move quickly and could only do so if they were operating from their 'portée' vehicle. On the portée, however, they were terribly conspicuous. The 2pdr detachments demonstrated repeatedly their self-sacrificing courage, but could not destroy enough tanks. As we have seen, the 25pdr was (in the desert) diverted to this task, for which it was unsuitable and in which it proved extremely vulnerable.

The 6pdr anti-tank gun appeared in the desert battles of 1942. It packed a bigger punch than the 2pdr and could thus open fire at longer range. It had a low silhouette and could quickly be dug-in and concealed. But in 1943 the German Tiger tank appeared and seemed to be proof against the 6pdr except at very close range. The British 17pdr was already available in small numbers and was able to kill the Tiger at 1,000 yards; it was distinctly less mobile than the 6pdr, and less easy to conceal, but for the rest of the war, except for one brief period, it held its own in the gun-tank battle. Both 6pdr and 17pdr were provided in due course with an ingenious form of shell called the discarding sabot, in which a light alloy casing, carrying the driving band, fell away at the muzzle after firing, leaving a streamlined shot to pursue its course to the target with enhanced velocity.

The term 'self-propelled gun' has always been somewhat misleading.

'Self-propulsion' was developed not merely to give the gun a mobile firing-platform — the portée did that — but to give it both self-contained mobility and also self-contained armoured protection. The 25pdr was an excellent gun, with a range of 13,500 yards, the ability to fire from behind hill-crests or other cover and (thanks to a 'platform', a form of horizontal wheel upon the rim of which stood the gun wheels) very quick to traverse from side to side against successive targets. In very mobile warfare field guns had to come into action in the open — no time to dig gunpits — and when their time came to move they had to move quickly; the so-called 'self-propelled' (SP) carriages were designed to meet these needs.

A series of SP field guns were produced, with ecclesiastical titles, Bishop, Priest and Sexton, the last of these — a 25pdr gun on a Canadian Ram tank chassis — giving distinguished service in Italy and North-west Europe. At the same time SP anti-tank guns appeared, first the Deacon — a 6pdr, with thick shield, on a four wheeled chassis — then a 3in gun on the American M10 chassis similar to that of the Sherman tank, then 17pdr guns on both the British Valentine tank chassis and on the M10. By the end of the war more than 50% of the divisional anti-tank artillery was self-propelled.

The man most responsible for the gunnery 'break-through', which, in the last few years of the war, at least tripled the value of artillery support in the British Army, was Brig Jack Parham. In an early chapter we mentioned his regimental concentration of 15 May 1940, when he was CO, 10th Field Regiment; its significance remained very much in his mind. After Dunkirk, however, impressed by the difficulties of exercising high-level control in the chaos of hurried retreat and in the fog of war, British military thought tended to favour small formations or unit columns, with batteries or even troops of guns supporting them. In the desert, as we have seen, similar developments occurred for rather different reasons.

Jack Parham knew this was wrong. Then, in 1940, he saw clearly that artillery fire, to be effective, needed to be concentrated in mass. Regimental concentrations, by 24 guns together, had been practised before the war, but the prescribed system of plotting and calculated checks made them slow affairs. Parham saw that we were trying to be too accurate with a weapon which (because of many variables in gun, shell, cartridge and meteorological conditions) would not produce pinpoint accuracy anyway. Because modern radio communication was more reliable and clear than before, it would permit a call for fire to reach many Gunner units within a few seconds. Omitting gunnery frills, therefore, a concentration of fire from all the 72 field guns of a division upon a single target should, within five minutes, smother an area around that target.

In 1941 Brig Parham was CRA 38th (Welsh) Division, in Dorset. After rehearsals seawards, he demonstrated at the School of Artillery and before a senior officers' course the system he had worked out. A volunteer from the spectators was invited to fire a mortar bomb on to any part of the artillery range confronting them — Parham instructed him quickly in the mortar's art — and the CRA's representative (one of Parham's COs) stood by to bring down the fire of 72 guns upon it within five minutes. Other targets were similarly treated and the School of Artillery and the rest of the audience persuaded to a man. Other demonstrations followed and, although in one of them the spectators suffered a 'near-miss', the system was accepted almost *en bloc*.

The necessary drills and instructions were quickly issued, with certain letters to indicate the number of guns called-upon to engage — 'Mike', for M, denoted a Regimental target for 24 guns, 'Uncle', for U, a Divisional

85
17pdr anti-tank gun — trial in the desert. *IWM*

86
Bishop — 25pdr on Valentine tank chassis — the first SP. *IWM*

87
Brig Jack Parham — tripled
the value of British field
artillery support.
Mrs Parham

88
Lt-Col Charles Bazeley, prime
evangelist of the Air OP.
*Royal Artillery Charitable -
Fund*

Artillery target for 72 guns; other letters would conjure even greater concentrations.

During 1942, as was mentioned in the last chapter, a feeling was arising in the desert that the tactics of using artillery in small packets was unsound and that artillery fire should be concentrated; as this view strengthened and as fresh commanders appeared to implement it, the 'Uncle Target' procedure was ready to hand. More than any other single factor, it won the war.

Another important gunnery development concerned observation of artillery fire from the air. During World War 1 the artillery of both sides was largely dependent on air observation for the correction of fire on to the target. The system was complex and slow, reliant on air-to-ground wireless and morse-code.

By 1934 this system had changed little, but in that year the Royal Artillery Flying Club was formed; Brig H. R. S. Massy was President, Capt Charles Bazeley Secretary, Jack Parham, needless to say, a member. These officers, and other members of the club, understood clearly the inadequacy of the present 'artillery co-operation' system to the mobile warfare for which the British Army was preparing. Instead of distantly based 'Army-coop' aircraft (with pilots only occasionally gunner officers seconded to the RAF) flying deep over enemy territory and dependant on speed for safety, they envisaged slow light aircraft, based in the artillery area, equipped with two-way speech-radio, piloted by professional gunners who would control artillery fire by means of normal gunnery methods and fire orders. Massy made the first approach to the War Office and, later, was posted to a senior appointment therein where he continued the struggle. Charles Bazeley was seconded to the RAF as a pilot in one of their Army Cooperation squadrons; he was the prime evangelist of the 'Air OP' concept, the key features of which were that observation would take place from points behind the 'front-line', climbing to observe and diving down for concealment, and that these small unarmed aircraft would survive by their manoeuvrability and by their very slowness.

As may be imagined, this was to the RAF dangerous heresy and progress was slow. Powerful support was forthcoming, however, from Sir Alan Brooke when C-in-C, Home Forces, and in August 1941 the first 'Air OP Squadron' started to form, with Bazeley as its commander. This and other such squadrons were RAF units but under artillery tactical control; while their servicing personnel were airmen, the pilots, signallers, transport drivers and commanders were Gunners. Equipped with Auster aeroplanes of successive marks, they were deployed in all major theatres of war, noteworthy initiators of 'Uncle Targets' and described by Field-Marshal Montgomery as 'a necessary part of gunnery'.

6 End of the Beginning

'This is not the end. It is not even the beginning of the end. But it is, perhaps, the end of the beginning.' — Winston Churchill, in the Mansion House, 10 November 1942.

In August 1942, with Rommel held on the El Alamein line, a change of command was made in the Middle East. Generals Sir Harold Alexander and Bernard Montgomery took over from Auchinleck as C-in-C and as Commander Eighth Army respectively. Montgomery at once sent for Sidney Kirkman as 'Brigadier Royal Artillery' (BRA) at his Army HQ. Kirkman had been Montgomery's BRA in England and had strong views on the planning and organisation of artillery support.

On 31 August Rommel made his last attempt to break through to Alexandria, commencing with a thrust south of the Alam el Halfa ridge. He was stopped, mainly by excellent anti-tank tactics, and withdrew; for two and a half months Montgomery prepared his counterblast.

The British plan was for a breakthrough by XXX Corps, after which X Corps's armour would pass through to ward off counter-attacks while XXX Corps extended its positions north and south and XIII Corps undertook diversions to the south. Great secrecy was observed in the planning and build-up stages, and must be adjudged successful since Rommel was on a visit to Germany when the battle started.

The artillery fire-plan, with which the Battle of El Alamein began at 9.30pm on 23 October 1942, received notable press publicity for it was the most spectacular affair of its kind since 1918. On the XXX Corps front of seven miles, 480 field and medium guns engaged the enemy artillery for 20 minutes at an intense rate of fire. Thereafter, as the infantry moved forward, accompanied by Gunner OP parties, the artillery concentrated their fire on all known or suspected enemy company areas and strong-points. A Gunner participant described the night's work as 'impressive at first, then exhausting, then rather maddening'; the ammunition numbers probably used more vigorous terms.

After nine days, in which Montgomery switched his attacks from one part of the battle-field to another, supported everywhere by as many guns as could be brought to bear, the final phase included for the Gunners two 'creeping-barrages', artillery fire programmes where the line of bursts moves forward in front of, and parallel to, the line of infantry. The final breakthrough was effected and on 3 November the pursuit began.

Capt Peter Barrington, then serving in D Battery of 3rd RHA, described in the *RA Commemoration Book* the breakthrough and pursuit:

'Then in clouds of thick, cloying dust, which was semi-solid up to one's waist, the Regiment disappeared into the gaps and every driver and every man peered forward to try to keep the next gun or truck in view. Battery commanders strove to keep up with battalion or regimental commanders, whose formations were pouring through the gaps and fanning out in a great flood. Men and officers alike were in a great state of excitement, disbelief and wonder.

'This was something quite new — large batches of disconsolate and dirty prisoners, batteries of enemy guns still in position pointing towards Cairo, with ammunition in plenty and all the sights intact. Fitters had a glorious time, and stores were rapidly filled with extra and undeclared bits and pieces which were to come in handy on the way to Tunis. There were numerous warnings about booby traps and the like, but it takes more than that to stop a Tiffy. Best of all, the enemy was not fighting back except on the coast road. Nothing could now hold the Army, and the 60th Rifles, with D Battery, among others, in support,

El Alamein

89
Brig Sidney Kirkman,
Montgomery's BRA. *IWM*
90
The opening artillery
preparation at El Alamein,
viewed from a forward OP.
IWM
91
The advance after the battle —
'brew-up' alongside a wrecked
Italian tank. *IWM*

made rapid progress parallel with the coast and about ten miles or so south of the road. The pace was too hot for many pauses, but on one occasion the Battery had a good shoot from the top of the escarpment overlooking an aerodrome. The Battery was brought into action without the FOO having the slightest idea where his guns were except that they were behind him — he hoped. No one knows to this day where the first shot went, but by taking a bearing back on to the sound of the gun firing, the Troop Commander gave a correction of 60 degrees and the next round appeared within 2 degrees of the enemy. It was one of those times when the FOO was quite glad the infantry Colonel was there to see, and he proceeded to shell the enemy out of range down the road by giving corrections and orders to fire in quick succession without waiting for the fall of shot — just the sort of shoot one used to practise for the benefit of visiting instructors at Larkhill.

'The chase continued every day and far into the night until the great column of Eighth Army men, now scornful of German and Italian alike, came in sight of the Egyptian barracks perched above Sollum.'

In the small hours of 8 November 1942 an Anglo-American force under Gen Eisenhower had landed in Morocco and Algeria and Gen K. A. Anderson's British First Army pushed east with the object of seizing Tunisia, and particularly the ports of Bizerta and Tunis. Anderson's BRA was Brig Jack Parham. His gunners had, we may be sure, been well grounded in the 'Uncle Target' procedures and under his control was Bazeley's No 651 Air OP Squadron, RAF. Parham was thus in the surely unprecedented position of carrying-out simultaneously the first battle evaluations of two of his own concepts.

Leading British units reached Medjez el Bab, a key objective 30 miles south-west of Tunis, on 25 November and three days later the minarets of Tunis were in view. But the Germans had reacted quickly and strongly; they had moved large quantities of armour by sea across the central Mediterranean and infantry by both sea and air; by 1 December the British were withdrawing. Free French and American forces were now operating to the south of First Army, however, and Anderson had by no means abandoned hope of concentrating his army well forward and breaking through to Tunis.

The first 'Uncle Target' shoots took place south of Medjez el Bab during indecisive fighting in January 1943. There was nothing indecisive about the shooting. The CRA of 6th Armoured Division had 86 guns, including Medium artillery, at his disposal; Lt-

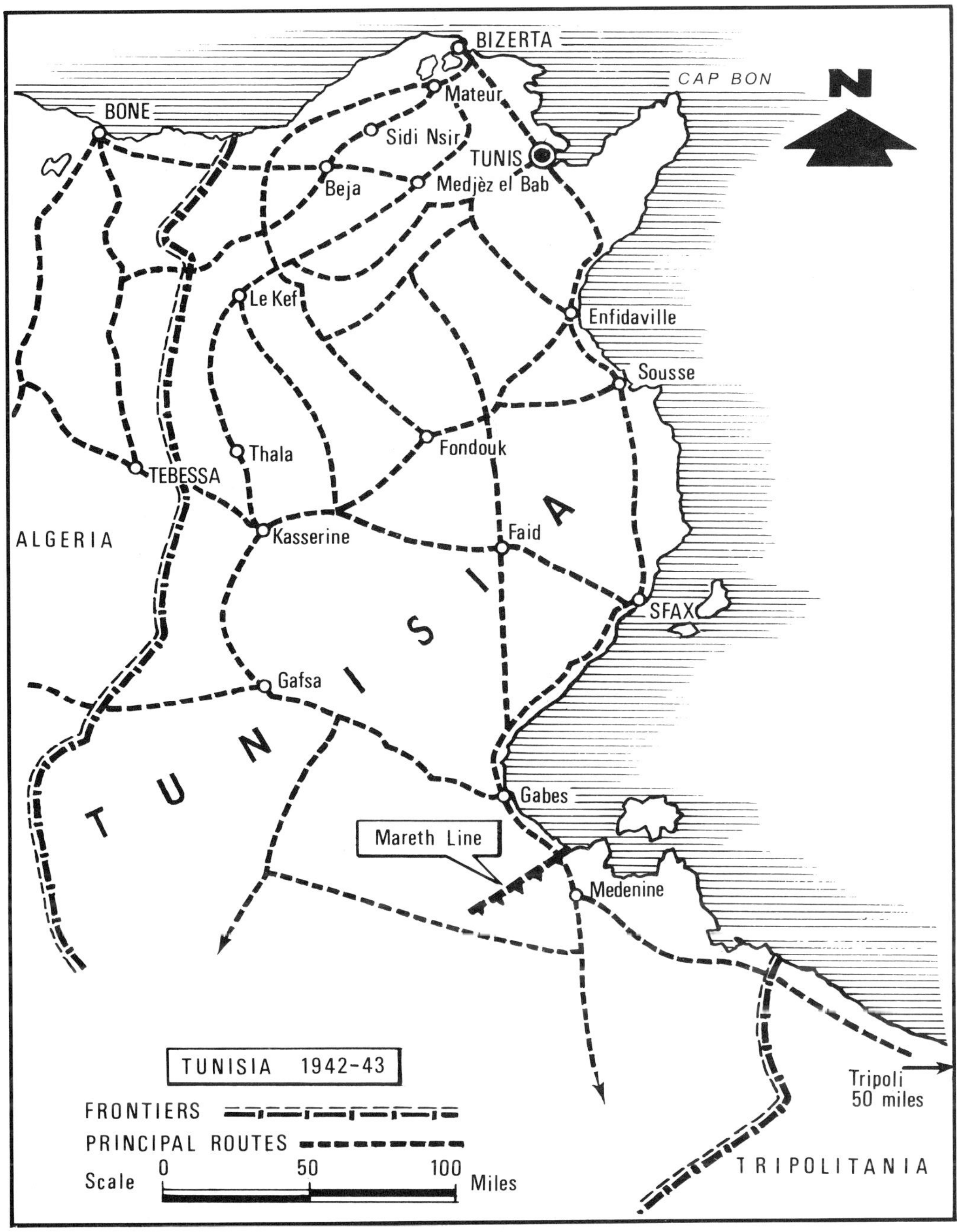

92
Tunisia, 1942-43.

93
First 'Uncle Target', Bou Arada, Tunisia, January 1943. German tanks after the battle. *IWM*

94
German Ju 88 shot down near Bou Arada, January 1943. *IWM*

93

94

Col J. A. T. Barstow, CO of 12th (Honourable Artillery Company) Regiment, RHA, saw from one of his OPs a group of 30 tanks and many 'soft' vehicles apparently engaged in an outflanking movement, called-for and was granted the whole of the divisional artillery and brought down devastating fire in accordance with the new artillery precepts. The CRA himself, Brig T. Lyon-Smith, then appeared, demanded his share of the fun and completed the discomfiture of the dispersed and withdrawing enemy with a further series of 'Uncle targets'.

In February the Germans launched a series of offensives, in succession from south to north. Rommel reappeared in the first of these, falling upon the United States' 1st Armoured Division, dispersed between Gafsa and Fondouk, on 14 February. This was a sad baptism of fire for the Americans who were driven through the Kasserine Pass in some confusion. American and British reinforcements stemmed the tide and Rommel turned back to rejoin his main force in the strong defences of the Mareth Line inside the Tunisian frontier with Tripolitania.

On the morning of 21 February Germans were moving through the Fondouk and Faid passes and 6th Armoured Division, whatever the lessons of the past, were forced to split tanks, infantry and guns into several small groups. One of these was 'Nick Force', commanded by Brig Cameron Nicholson, a Gunner by profession but at that time second-in-command of the division. Nick Force then consisted of two armoured regiments and something over a battalion of infantry, together with F Battery of 12th (HAC) Regiment, RHA; it adopted a blocking position east of Thala on the road leading north to Le Kef.

Soon after dark enemy tanks appeared a hundred yards in front of one of F Battery's troop positions and were repulsed with the destruction of three of them. Gradually it became apparent that their advanced infantry had been overrun and that F Battery and C Company of 10th Rifle Brigade were now in the front line. Much digging took place during the night and an OP was established on the left flank of the position, manned by Capt I. Buchanan (an attached Canadian officer).

The following account of the day's events was written by Maj C. Middleton, the Battery Commander, for the *RA Commemoration Book*:

'The area was shelled at frequent intervals throughout the morning and several tanks which appeared on the crest about 1,500 to 3,000 yards away were engaged furiously over open sights. When AP ran short, HE 119 ''cap-on'' was used. It is doubtful if any of the tanks were actually knocked out but they were certainly discouraged. OPs were also engaged over open sights. No infantry attack on the position developed during the day, but the shelling was heavy and obviously directed from the ridge in front, and casualties amounted to one killed and thirteen wounded, including Captain Pirie, who had been an inspiration throughout. During the day the battery was greatly heartened by a visit from the BRA, First Army, Brigadier Parham, who insisted on visiting each gun. While he was there a German motorcyclist with sidecar advanced down the ridge in front and after having been greeted with a hail of ill-directed small-arms fire was knocked out by a gun. Too late, and to our great regret, we discovered that he was a medical orderly who had clearly lost his way.

'The road from Thala was under shellfire and during the day the quads had to run the gauntlet several times to bring up more ammunition. The evacuation of casualties was undertaken voluntarily by Gunners Kerr and Peters, the driver and wireless operator of one of the troop leader's trucks. They worked untiringly, often under shellfire, and succeeded in getting all casualties, both our own and those of other nearby units, back to the ADS at Thala.

'Another highlight of the day was Captain Buchanan's OP work. Practically all the time his line was out of action, as it was repeatedly cut by shellfire, but he was able to carry on sending fire orders by ''voice control'', which he enlivened with suitable words of encouragement. When his voice failed him he engaged enemy OPs with his rifle and claimed several hits. By the end of the day he could no longer speak. We were told later that his running commentary had been a great encouragement to a company of the Rifle Brigade who, unknown to us, had been in a position on our right.'

During the battle the artillery of the 9th United States Division began to

95
Victim of a 6pdr detachment of
229 Battery of 58 Anti-tank
Regiment
IWM
96
After the battle, Gen Anderson
and Brig 'Cam' Nicholson.
IWM

arrive, followed by 152nd Field Regiment, RA, and other reinforcements, and the enemy began to withdraw.

On 24 February the third German thrust was well under way, by an armoured battle group with upwards of 70 tanks including their new Mark VI tank (Tiger) which had first appeared in this theatre in January. Their way was blocked by 128th Brigade of 46th Infantry Division at a narrow break in the hills, known as Hunt's Gap, about five miles north of the road junction at Beja, itself 25 miles west of Medjez-el-Bab. An outpost position had been established at Sidi Nsir, a little village surrounded by hills and about 12 miles in front of the Brigade position. Here stood the 5th Hampshires and the 25pdrs of 155th Battery of 172nd Field Regiment, Maj John Raworth being the Battery Commander.

There were two alternative enemy approach routes, along the railway from the north-east and along the road from the east; the Hampshires manned the commanding heights, accompanied by Gunner OPs, the guns were in two troop positions south (E Troop) and north (F Troop) of the Mateur road. A

minefield had been laid each side of the road to the east of the position.

Brig W. D. McN. Graham, who at that time commanded 172nd Field Regiment, wrote for the *RA Commemoration Book* an account of the battle which followed, from which the following extract is taken:

'Soon after 6 a.m. on February 26th F Troop came under fire from mortars behind Chechak Ridge and replied with artillery fire. From this moment until dark, F Troop and to a lesser degree E Troop and the command posts, cooks' shelters, etc, were under increasingly heavy mortar fire. At 7 a.m. enemy tanks attempted a direct assault down the main road from Mateur. F Troop engaged them, No 1 gun over open sights. Three tanks were hit and the road was blocked very conveniently just where it passed through a protective minefield. No 1 gun remained in action in spite of mortar and machine-gun fire . . .

'At 9.40 a.m. Point 609 was heavily attacked by infantry. Communications were broken, WT sets smashed by enemy mortars and all lines cut. Lieutenant McGee was wounded and taken prisoner . . . From this moment on, the battery had but secondary "eyes" overlooking the Mateur road, which must have been packed with enemy tanks and vehicles.

'At 10.15 the CO visited Major Raworth on the gun position. F Troop was then under observation at a range of about 800 yards, and the track leading down to the command post was under very heavy and accurate mortar fire, rounds falling every three seconds or so. On all eight guns the CO found the detachments full of cheerful and determined courage. Lieutenant Taylor and Sergeant Henderson (both of F Troop) in particular stood out by reason of their undaunted offensive spirit and the inspiring example they set. Sergeant Henderson was the No 1 of No 1 gun, specially placed on the top of the slope to deal with enemy tanks trying to use the Mateur-Sidi Nsir road. Taylor was the only officer on F Troop position, and he fought there until he was killed.

'At this time Messerschmidts attacked from a height of about 200 feet and raked the gun positions with machine-gun and cannon fire. A number of vehicles were burning along the road Sidi Nsir — Hunt's Gap, some of them filled with ammunition and ammonal; but the risks were ignored by officers and men alike as they cheerfully salvaged and carried the shells throughout the action. The wounded acted stoically; none grumbled or complained.

'By noon enemy tanks (reported to number 30) and infantry had wormed their way into positions around the flanks of the guns. All this time the battery was completely occupied in engaging enemy infantry, machine-guns and mortars, which were closing in on the Hampshire company positions.

'The battery fired as many as 1,800 rounds per gun during that fierce, relentless day. Bren guns claimed four Messerschmidts — a triumphant reward for days and days of patient shooting on the balloon range at Lydd before leaving England.

'The gallantry of the infantry, isolated on the tops of stony djebels, was superb. Both artillery and infantry were equally determined not to let their opposite numbers down.

'At 3 p.m. a column of enemy infantry penetrated between Hampshire Farm, two miles or so to the west of the Sidi Nsir - Beja road, and the gun positions, and no more ammunition could pass. Twenty minutes later, under covering fire from some 13 tanks in hull-down positions (firing MGs and guns), more tanks attempted to advance down the main road. A Panzer Mk VI was leading. This was hit three times by Sergeant Henderson's gun. A smaller Panzer Mk IV tried to pass, but this in turn was knocked out by No 1 gun. Yet a third tank was set on fire by the same gun.

'The enemy held back, shelling and machine-gunning the positions, particularly F Troop, which was more easily spotted. Both troops were now in action against enemy tanks over open sights. But the tanks in hull-down positions had a great advantage over our guns and engaged them one by one, setting on fire ammunition dumps, killing or wounding the detachments and smashing up the guns themselves.

'At four o'clock another attack was put in from the Mateur road against F Troop's southern flank. Sergeant Henderson smashed up the leading tank, but immediately afterwards he and his entire detachment were knocked out by a direct hit . . . The tanks then came on over the ridge in front of F Troop, who still had three guns in action and engaged the enemy at ranges from 50 to 10 yards with Lieutenant Taylor, the fitter, cooks and all survivors running from gun to gun and servicing each in turn.

'At this stage the slope of the ground, which is steep and convex, gave the gunners some much-needed help, for the attacking tanks were handicapped by their limited ability to depress their guns. F Troop fired for over an hour more before they were finally silenced. Then the tanks moved down the road past F Troop and surrounded E Troop.'

The last throes of E Troop are described in the following extract from an article by Lt-Cdr G. S. Stavert in the *British Army Review* of December 1977. The writer took part in the battle as an officer of E Troop.

'A row of turrets appeared along the crest, and the world erupted in a jarring, shattering burst of noise as everything opened at once. It was impossible to distinguish the noise of exploding shells from that of the 25-pounders firing back. The air was filled with horrid little red streaks of tracer. In addition to its 88mm gun, each tank carried two machine-guns. These they used to spray the whole area, with distinctly demoralising effect. A row of little holes appeared across the top of the shield of No 3 gun. The sergeant yelled at his men to keep their heads down as they strove to break all records for reloading. They fired, and then he yelled again as the solid shot, its trajectory clearly revealed by its red spark of tracer, struck the front of a Tiger tank a glancing blow and went careering off into space. With hull-down targets and only a frontal shot he had next to no chance of making a kill. I ran down the ditch to No 4. Tracer flew overhead and spat into the ground just like it did on the practice evolutions at battle camp — only these fellows weren't firing on fixed lines. But No 4 was already out of action, leaning untidily on a smashed trunnion in the middle of a pile of burning ammunition. Outside the pit a group of figures lay prone and still on the ground.

'Back at No 3 there were still men working in the pit, though the shield was now looking like the top of a pepper-pot. A high velocity shell hit the corner of the Command Post just by my ear. I saw the flash and heard the crack but didn't feel the blast at all. I thought, "Poor sods, they've all had it in there", and immediately in the same breath, "Serve 'em right for not being out here". A gunner of No 2 collapsed, shot through both ankles. Another on No 3 fell into the ditch, his face completely covered in blood. His mate tumbled down beside him, horror-struck.

' "What shall I do? What shall I do?" he kept asking.

' "Stay with him," I said. It was the wrong thing to say, but it seemed the best answer at the time.

'Over on the right a most extraordinary thing was happening.

The sergeant of No 1 gun, intent like the rest on firing up the slope, had failed completely to observe that the main body of the tank force was coming down upon them by the road. The leading tank was already round the corner, not ten yards away from his gun muzzle. Its turret was open, the commander leaning out of it, pistol in hand, not bothering to fire. You could almost see the grin on his face.

'Yet still the covering tanks lay back on the crest and pounded at the weakening troop. Each gun-pit was now a circle of flames wherein Dante-esque figures ducked and lay, as one after another the open boxes of cordite charges burst like giant Roman candles, sending columns of black smoke upwards, tinged with red. A direct hit on No 3 had folded up its shield like a piece of wet blotting-paper. The remainder of the detachment, incredibly still alive, tumbled into the ditch. I tumbled in after them. The last gun had ceased firing, and a seemingly endless queue of Mark IVs, led by a Tiger, rolled slowly nose to tail across our front. If anything looked like moving, they shot it up. There seemed no limit to the prodigality of their ammunition. A blazing Bren carrier, long since abandoned, lay useless at the roadside with a tank not ten yards away still squirting bullets into it for all he was worth.

'Slowly the leading tanks rumbled on down the hill towards the station, and the shooting died down. It was dark, save for the light from the fires. Half a dozen sand-coloured tanks with palm-tree emblems painted on their sides were halted just above us. Figures were getting out of them, beckoning. Figures, too, were emerging from the bowels of the earth, out of the wreckage of the broken Command Posts and the gun-pits. The dead men from No 4 got up and staggered towards the road, two of them leaning on the shoulders of the others. The BSM came by, ruin and despair written all over his face; . . . The BC was there, too, with a German Officer.

' "Come along, everybody," he called. "There's nothing more we can do now." '

The night that followed was significant in two ways. The enemy paused and licked his wounds and the heavens opened for days of torrential rain. The valley to the Hunt's Gap position

Sidi Nsir, February 1943

97
Disabled German tank on the battlefield. *IWM*
98
Maj John Raworth, OC 155 Field Battery. *Mrs Raworth*

became a morass in which the tanks floundered. Heavy reinforcements, including medium artillery, reached 128th Brigade. The enemy's tanks were bombarded in the valley and their infantry on the bare hills; the enemy too were reinforced but on 2 March, at the first sign of a British counter-offensive, they withdrew, abandoning 30 tanks.

To what extent one may relate the success at Hunt's Gap to the day's delay and punishment imposed by 155th Battery and the 5th Hampshires at Sidi Nsir is hard to prove. One must simply quote from the formal submission after the battle of Lt-Col, H. C. C. Newnham of the Hampshires: 'I voice the feelings of my Battalion when I can only recommend that 155th Battery receive the highest award for valour. Their unshaken devotion to the guns was an epic and as gun by gun was silenced so did survivors make their way to help the guns remaining in action.'

The Eighth Army had entered Tripoli on 23 January 1943, 7th Armoured Division following the enemy across the Tunisian frontier up to the outpost positions east of the Mareth Line. On 17 February Medenine was captured, together with the Tajera Hills to the north-west of it. As the port of Tripoli was opened by degrees to shipping, more troops moved west, including 51st Highland Division which occupied a sector between the Tajera and the coast and the New Zealand Division deployed to the south of 7th Armoured Division. An enemy attack was expected and it was likely to be primarily an armoured one. General Montgomery foretold its date as 5 March and, with full confidence in

his soothsaying powers, the intervening period was spent in the most complete and thorough planning of the Medenine defences.

After some controversy, eventually umpired by the Army Commander, it was decided that the anti-tank guns (including those of the infantry battalions as well as those of the artillery batteries) should be deployed in a single 'lay-out', designed not for local anti-tank defence but to kill tanks. The three British and one New Zealand anti-tank regiments (57th, 65th, 73rd and 7th New Zealand) totalled 256 guns, all 6pdrs save for a few of the new 17pdrs deployed inconspicuously in the rear areas of the New Zealand Division. Infantry anti-tank guns brought the total to 472, of which only 48 were 2pdrs.

West of Tarhuna on the Tripoli road, 25 or 26 January 1943. Bofors of 15 LAA Regiment just after an engagement. *IWM*

100
Tripoli. Churchill inspects 64 Medium Regiment. CO, with Churchill, is Lt-Col M. Yates, behind them Lord Alanbrooke. *IWM*

100

The field and medium artillery (3rd and 5th RHA, 4th, 53rd, 58th, 97th, 111th and 146th Field, 4th, 5th, 6th New Zealand Field and 7th, 64th and 69th Medium Regiments) had registered a very large number of targets and were ready to engage as 'Mike (regimental) targets' any unregistered target that appeared. Provision was made for CsRA, Infantry, Tanks and linked Gunner regiments to call down concentrations as required. The Tajera provided good OPs; it also conveniently accommodated Bofors guns of 15th LAA Regiment. Very few mines were laid, but lavish dummy minefields were prepared to canalise enemy tank formations.

On 6 March, after preliminary activity in 51st Division's sector, the enemy's first main attack came at daylight, directed against 131st Queen's Brigade, 201st Guards Brigade and later 5th New Zealand Brigade. Four such attacks were launched during the day, each preceded by Stuka dive-bombers.

In the first attack the tanks led, followed by infantry. Maj-Gen R. F. K. Belchem, who was CO 1st Royal Tank Regiment on this day, has written in the *Royal Artillery Journal* of September 1976:

'The overall leading wave comprised 80 tanks and three battalions of Panzer Grenadiers. By 0930, reserve battle-groups were committed by the Germans on all sectors. The German tanks, by around 0945, had sustained (brewed-up or immobilised) the loss of 28 out of 115 committed. One anti-tank 6-pr gun of the 131 Brigade destroyed

101
Medenine, 6 March 1943,
6pdr of 73 Anti-tank Regiment
with, beyond, disabled enemy
tanks. *Royal Artillery Charitable Fund*

102
7.2in howitzer firing, Tunisia,
56 Heavy Regiment (Spike
Milligan's own). *IWM*

five enemy tanks in the first hour of the battle, and 73 Anti-Tank Regiment accounted for at least four on the New Zealand front. The importance of the dummy minefields at this stage should be noted.

'The assault infantry debussed in a reasonably orderly fashion, for there was an almost traditional silence from the British lines until the foremost anti-tank guns opened up. But thereafter there came down a devastating volume of field and medium gunfire on the Panzer Grenadiers. They were pinned down, dispersed, and suffered very heavy casualties. In no section were they able to get to grips with our FDLs. Meanwhile, the tank groups had suffered a one-in-four casualty rate and, conscious that the infantry were not able to advance through them, had no alternative to withdrawal; to remain forward would have meant complete destruction from short-range anti-tank fire.

'Thus the tanks pulled back to reform, and the infantry leaders gathered their survivors as best they could.'

Second and third attacks, at about 10am and 2.30pm respectively, were dealt-with in the same manner. A penetration of the dummy minefield was made, however, at the cost of bunching and presenting good targets to the field artillery.

The fourth attack, at about 5pm, differed from the others in two respects; it advanced far enough for two troops of Belchem's tanks to be deployed against it and German infantry succeeded in penetrating the Queen's Brigade's position. A dusk counter-attack, with full artillery support, ejected them. The Stukas, and other enemy aircraft, meanwhile, had had a rugged time from the light anti-aircraft gunners who produced, in Rommel's own words, 'an AA screen of hitherto unparalleled intensity'.

At the end of the fourth attack the Panzers had had enough; two radio intercepts, from the 15th and 21st Panzer Divisions, painted the picture:

'It is quite impossible to continue'.

'We cannot again attack in these conditions'.

Rommel ordered withdrawal to the Mareth Line. This was not so easy, however. Avoidance of anti-tank and small arms fire had distributed the tanks in concentrated groups in the dead ground, their crews striving to get organised and to repair damaged or immobilised tanks. Here they were visited by torrential rain and continual British harassing fire. After midnight sounds of tank movement were heard and tremendous artillery concentrations brought down on the well-registered enemy harbour-areas.

Col G. P. Gregson, who commanded

5th RHA in this battle, describes in the *RA Commemoration Book* its final stage:

'Patrols pushed out at first light and more than confirmed our wildest hopes. A complete withdrawal had taken place and some 800 yards from our position a grotesque tank cemetery was found — tank piled against tank, crews slumped over the wreckage, and indications of desperation and panic where all tactical conception had vanished in an endeavour to avoid the devastating fire of our anti-tank gunners. Terrible carnage had been wrought by well-directed artillery concentrations into this shambles during the previous day and more especially during the night. The movement we had heard during the night was an

103
Priest 105mm SP gun of 11 RHA, south of Medjez-el-Bab, April 1943. *IWM*

104
Bishop 25pdr SP guns, probably of 12 RHA (HAC), near Medjez-el-Bab, April 1943. *IWM*

105
3.7in gun of 208 HAA Battery in action south of Medjez-el-Bab, April 1943. *IWM*

106
Auster III, 654 Air OP Squadron, taking-off — Tunisia April 1943. *IWM*

attempted evacuation, but artillery fire had made this almost impossible, and we found many tanks almost intact amongst the total bag of 52. Our casualties in anti-tank guns and men had not been heavy and we had lost only one tank to achieve one of the most decisive victories in North Africa.'

Tunisia was the first operational testing ground of the Air Observation Posts. It was a stern test, because the enemy had, at first, air superiority and secondly because the Auster aeroplane with which No 651 Squadron was equipped was no more than a training aircraft, without landing-flaps or self-sealing petrol tanks and with a poor backward view from the pilot's seat. The air OPs were quickly plunged into a hurried advance followed by a withdrawal. In the first fortnight, with the eight available aircraft, thirty-seven sorties had been flown; only twice had an aircraft been attacked and only one pilot lost, Capt A. H. Newton, shot-down by Messerschmitt 109s while approaching to land. By February 1943 the squadron was complete with aircraft and Charles Bazeley, the squadron commander, went home to pass the operational know-how to succeeding squadrons.

The Air OPs had proved themselves. On 4 March No 654 Squadron, with operational Auster IIIs, arrived in the theatre and was allotted to Eighth Army.

Between 20 and 23 March Eighth Army attacked and then outflanked the Mareth Line. Rommel withdrew to a position thirty miles north-west, whence he personally was withdrawn to Germany. His successor, the Italian Gen Messe, withdrew further to a strong position at Enfidaville, 150 miles south of Tunis. Gen Alexander now commanded all the Allied land forces in Tunisia; AM Coningham was the overall air force commander and air superiority belonged to the Allies. For the last battle in North Africa the most intense concentration of artillery was achieved and the most detailed preparations made, including wholesale 'dumping' of ammunition. The offensive, starting on 6 May, was almost an anticlimax. On the following afternoon British tanks entered Tunis and on the 9th were on the Cap Bon peninsula. By the 12th, 250,000 Germans and Italians had laid down their arms.

107
German Mark VI tank (Tiger) knocked-out by 17pdr in the final battle in Tunisia. *IWM*

107

7 Jungle Green

On 7 December 1941, with its sudden attack on Pearl Harbour, the United States naval base in Hawaii, Japan entered the war on the Axis side. As a result the immense strength of the American nation was thrown into the scales on the opposite side and, in the end, proved a decisive factor in the Allied victory. It was almost three years, however, before such victory, in the Far East, began to appear an imminent possibility; meanwhile exiguous British forces had to suffer similar bitter experiences to those of their counterparts in Europe. The island of Hong Kong, isolated and relatively defenceless, fell on Christmas Day. Simultaneously, aided by heavy attacks on British airfields, the sinking of the warships *Prince of Wales* and *Repulse* and the small numbers and archaic equipment of the forces opposing them, however gallantly, the Japanese pushed down the Malayan peninsula towards the island of Singapore.

This island had recently been heavily fortified against seaward attack, its defences including three 15in coast artillery guns. These had, of course, been sited, and ammunition provided, against the eventuality of attack from the sea, not an enemy advance through Malaya, and this has often led to the allegation that the guns were so sited that they could not fire in the landwards direction. Maj Jim Nelson was, in 1941, Brigade Major to Brig E. W. Goodman, the senior artillery officer in Malaya Command. He relates how he was informed that it was not possible to fire these guns landwards but that a re-routeing of the guns' power supply soon resolved that difficulty. He goes on:

'In due course I selected targets on the mainland for the 15-inch guns which, of course, had certain limitations when used in a "ground" role — from their flat trajectories and thus lack of pin-point accuracy, and from ammunition designed to sink ships rather than devastate a land area. I was, probably rightly, refused permission to engage the Sultan of Johore's palace (a most tempting target) since, I was told, the Sultan had paid for the guns! So I selected a railway yard in the same area. An Australian Gunner officer was appointed to observe the fire and a telephone link established direct from him to me in Fort Canning.

'The first three-gun salvo of 15-inch shells was quite something — like three express trains roaring overhead — most impressive, but for quite a time no reaction from the observer. After what seemed an interminable wait a highly excited Australian reported to the tune, "It's terrific — magnificent — those

108
15in coast gun at Singapore.
IWM

109
Indian Mountain Artillery section (3.7in howitzer) near Shwegyin, North Burma, May 1942. *IWM*

110
Arakan, 1943-44.

shells must have burrowed deep into Johore before the fuses went-off. Whole chunks of land have now come up, hurling trains, engines and trucks high in the air. More, please! It's marvellous''.'

These guns, and the other coast artillery guns which also engaged landward targets, were not, nor could they have been, a decisive factor in the defence of Singapore under the prevailing conditions. The field artillery which had fought in Malaya continued to fight on the island and were almost out of ammunition when, on 15 February 1942, the garrison had finally to capitulate.

The Japanese, meanwhile, were overrunning the Philippine Islands, the Dutch East Indies and Borneo, had landed in New Guinea and, in January 1942, had entered Burma from Thailand. They outmanoeuvred British-Indian forces between the Salween River and Rangoon and set them into a disastrous withdrawal which only ended in May inside Assam on India's north-eastern frontier. Of the 150 British guns in Burma, only 25 survived this retreat.

The last guns in action were the four surviving Bofors of 3rd Indian LAA Battery (Maj Charles MacFetridge) on 10 May, at Shwegyin on the east bank of the River Chindwin, 5 miles south of Kalewa. Supporting the rearguard of 16th Indian Infantry Brigade, this

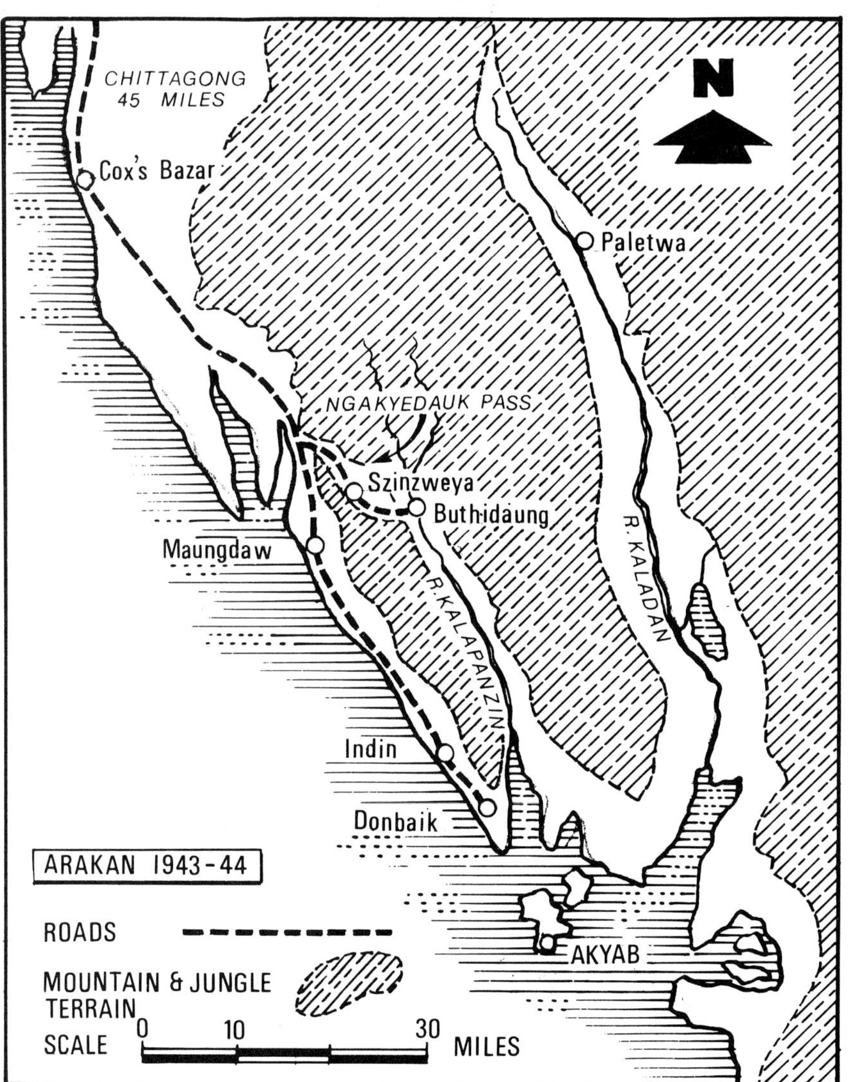

Battery engaged, all that day, not only Japanese aircraft but also, over open sights, their artillery, mortars and infantry — first to cover the embarkation on river-craft of tanks, troops and casualties and then, when these craft could no longer operate, to cover the withdrawal of the final rear parties, east of the river, to a crossing-place further north.

The guns could not use this route and had finally to be destroyed. At about 8pm a last tremendous concentration was fired by the battery, of which the *Official History* (HMSO) quoted an infantry war diary: 'The chief contribution came from the Bofors whose tracer shells lit up the descending darkness. It was a cheering sound, the like of which we had not heard during our time in Burma.'

Still more important than the moral-effect, was the uncharacteristic failure of the Japanese to follow-up and interfere with the subsequent withdrawal.

The artillery in India now faced difficulties more daunting than those of the Royal Artillery in Britain after Dunkirk, and by no means confined to the replacement of guns and other equipment.

Field artillery had to find gun positions in jungle, but still with a 'field of fire', and they needed to be defended against infiltrating 'gun-busting parties', a Japanese speciality. The 25pdr gun was still of service, though with a shorter axle; the 3.7in mountain howitzer, however, tried weapon of the Indian artillery, designed to be 'broken-down' into mule or human loads but also towed by 'jeeps', was the most useful field artillery weapon in the theatre. The 3in mortar was also introduced into some gunner batteries. Medium and heavy artillery were eventually provided in small quantities and used, among other roles, to destroy Japanese 'bunkers' (dug-in defended posts), often at very short range with direct-laying.

The methods being evolved in Britain and latterly the Middle East for the quick concentration of artillery fire had obvious limitations in thick jungle but they were well understood and were ready to be applied when conditions permitted.

The Japanese, in phase with their advance through central Burma and up to the Assam frontier, had occupied the Arakan coast of north-west Burma, including Akyab Island with its port and airfield. The 14th Indian Division was given the task (in the light of subsequent events somewhat optimistic) of recapturing it. Setting out from the Chittagong area in September 1942 it had, by the end of the year, established itself between Maungdaw and Buthidaung, across the jungle-covered Mayu mountain range. By early February 1943, two brigades had reached, at Donbaik, the final Japanese positions north of Akyab, and an amphibious operation was contemplated to capture the latter.

Instead, at the end of March, the Japanese took the offensive, first advancing north up the valley of the River Mayu and then infiltrating west over the mountain range, in rear of the 47th Indian and 6th British Brigades which were east and west, respectively, of the range. 6th Brigade had formed a 'lay-back' position covering Kyaukpandu, near the coast and about 15 miles north of Akyab, and both brigades sent back parties to clear their communications. The Japanese

111
AA Battery on the Assam-Burma frontier during the monsoon, 1943. *IWM*

112
Ammunition-supply — normal method. *IWM*

brushed aside the 47th Brigade parties, crossed the Mayu range and looked down upon 6th Brigade on the coastal plain. What followed is, perhaps, representative of many isolated engagements in Burma in which small Gunner detachments did all possible to support their infantry.

By the morning of 5 April the 6th Infantry Brigade Group, under Brig R. V. C. Cavendish, had withdrawn from the Donbaik position to a strip of coast, about seven miles long and never more than a mile wide, with their lay-back position at its north end manned by the 1st Berkshires and 12 25pdrs of 130th Field Regiment, RA. The other three battalions of the brigade, 1st Royal Scots, 2nd Durham Light Infantry and 1st Royal Welsh Fusiliers were in the Indin area and the remaining guns, 12 25pdrs of 494th Field Battery and four jeep-drawn 3.7in howitzers of 472nd Battery attached from 99th Field Regiment, RA, together with a company of the DLI and a small party of Jat machine gunners, were in the Kwason area three miles south of Indin. In a copse, between infantry and artillery, extraordinarily isolated, was the brigade commander and his head-quarters.

During the afternoon of 5 April the DLI and RWF attacked Japanese in the hills to the east and reported some pro-gress. The Commanding Officer of 130th Field Regiment, Lt-Col Ronald Nicholson (brother of Cameron, of Nickforce in Tunisia) attended Brig Cavendish's 'orders' and returned to his own HQ. At about 8.30 there was the sound of firing to the north, the gunners stood-to, the firing ceased. At 4.30am on the 6th Nicholson was aroused to speak by telephone with the Brigadier who told him that Brigade HQ was surrounded and the end was near; Nicholson was now in command of all troops south of Brigade HQ and was to instruct the CO of the DLI to take command of the brigade's infantry, to clear the Brigade HQ area and to open a way north for the guns.

Nicholson passed these orders and at dawn carried out a reconnaissance. He observed Japanese in the Brigade HQ area and Brig Cavendish under escort. Then Maj Awdrey of 472 Battery appeared and established an OP alongside Nicholson. His 3.7in how-itzers opened-up on the area surround-ing Brigade HQ and flushed out many Japanese, who moved towards the hills. It was evident, however, that some remained and that Japanese units in the foothills were moving round the right flank of Nicholson's position.

The DLI company and an OP of 494 Field Battery moved out to the right flank to delay the Japanese enveloping movement, while preparations were made to 'break-out' north from Indin at 3pm, the earliest time they could cross a chaung (stream) running out to sea. A smoke screen was arranged with the guns in the lay-back position and the crew of every vehicle would fire, as they passed, at the 'Brigade HQ' copse. Nicholson, in a *Royal Artillery Journal* article of January 1949, con-tinues as follows:

'The column started to form-up in the trees at Kwason. Mike Lawrence, still out in his carrier and exhausted with malaria, stuck to his job and increased the rate of fire. The first guns came out of action. At 1445 we tested the chaung and selected the best place to cross. It was just possible. The guns in the north started their smoke screen, the cases of the smoke shells falling near our Start Point. Soon a good "fog of war" was formed, and with a cheer the first vehicle passed Major Awdrey, now controlling the start, crossed the improvised road and made for the chaung.

'Would it cross or stick? It was a carrier, and mistaking the marked crossing place, it stuck. This looked like being the last straw, and to make matters worse Jap mortar bombs began to fall in the vicinity. The next vehicle approached the right spot, the gunners leaned out with their rifles at the "ready". If ever men prayed hard, we who watched did then.

'Lurching and heaving, the good old "Quad" waded through, and the gunners, yelling like mad, opened fire with their rifles as they passed the ill-fated copse. Again we stood, our hearts in our mouths, to see if there was any retaliation. In the din going on it was not possible to distinguish shots, but the gun and quad went on and passed out of sight round a bend in the shore. The rest of the column filed by, every-one at the top of his form; even the four Jat machine gunners, completely bewildered, grinned back and waved to us as they got ready to fire their Vickers guns over the side of their truck.

'Two vehicles on their last legs had, on arrival at Kwason, broken down completely and the flames of their funeral pyre now lit up the scene. The smoke screen continued to be fired by Major Charles Laughton, commanding the guns in the north, the officers and gunners loading and firing for over an hour to keep it going. By 1615hrs. the last vehicles, marching men and mules were on their way. Our little rearguard of carriers was waiting. We did our best to destroy the few vehicles which had stuck in the chaung. Mike Lawrence, firing until the Japs were within 1,500 yards of the guns and keeping them off till the last, had gone by with his troops.'

Having passed the former Brigade HQ the guns of A Troop of 315 Battery and P Troop of 494 Battery, now in view of the Japanese in the foothills 800 yards to the east, came into action. Firing over open sights, the gunners engaged the enemy with every kind of ammunition, including smoke and armour-piercing shell. Men, mules and vehicles moved on to the north under cover of this fire.

Nicholson continues, evidently reminded of a classic Gunner exploit of the battle of Fuentes d'Onoro, 132 years before:
'Then occurred the great moment of this hectic day. The DLI, RWF, and R.Scots, weary and exhausted, moving out from Indin to the beach in their disciplined and well ordered columns began to file past in the rear of the guns. The sight of the Gunners, now under fire from the Japs, sending shell after shell in retaliation was too much for the magnificent discipline of the Infantry. Taking off their helmets they broke ranks and rushed up to the guns. As in 1811 "An English shout arose", but on this 6th April, 1943, it was a British cheer — from Englishmen, Scotsmen and Welshmen — which rolled out over the Bay of Bengal above the din of battle. Cheering the gunners again and again and clapping them on their backs the infantry showed, in this spontaneous action, their appreciation of the co-operation given by the men of the Royal Regiment.
'After all that had happened, causing sadness, depression and a feeling of despair at our own losses and inability to defeat the Japs, here was one occasion where the grit and "guts" of the British soldier could overcome the apparently invincible yellow-faced Jap. With their steel helmets tilted on the back of their heads, sweat pouring off their faces, the gunners in their dirty begrimed khaki drill battledress (jungle green was still unheard of) swearing as only a British soldier can swear, grinned and went on loading and firing. The infantry reformed and marched on, the RWF leaving some carriers to protect the guns. When the last shell had been fired the gunners, revving up the "Quads", limbered up and went on their way rejoicing that they had at last defeated Colonel Tanahashi and his redoubtable troops of 112 Japanese Regiment, and lived again to fight another day with the 25-pdrs they had brought through to safety.'

Brief reference was previously made to Lt-Col Wingate's part in the Ethiopian campaign. This Gunner officer now appeared in the Burma picture, General Wavell having sent for him to advise on the prospect of guerilla operations there. Wingate advocated 'long-range penetration' (LRP) operations to disrupt Japanese south-to-north communications — supported by an offensive by the Allied main force.

Such offensive in fact proved impracticable but Wavell and Wingate agreed that the operation of the 'Chindits' (as they came to be called) should proceed without it, to test the concept and particularly the large scale and regular air supply upon which it depended. In February and March 1943 the Chindits succeeded in cutting the Japanese rail link to north Burma; thereafter they encountered severe difficulties and dispersed into small groups which reached India or China with many casualties. Wingate was summoned to England by Churchill and taken with the British Chiefs-of-Staff to an Anglo-American conference at Quebec. There his concept of another LRP operation, this time by a force of six brigades, was accepted and the C-in-C of the India-Burma theatre (now Gen Auchinleck) instructed to raise the necessary force.

Once again the supporting offensives by the main forces failed to materialise. The Chindits were launched however, in February and March 1944, into the areas in rear of the coming Japanese offensive. 'Strongholds' were established deep in jungle, equipped by air with artillery from 69th LAA and 160th Field Regiments. By 24 March three brigades were deployed across the Japanese south-to-north communications. But on

24 March Wingate was killed in an aircraft crash; his plans were changed and his Chindits badly mishandled. Wingate's reputation too has been mishandled by writers of the 1950s and later. We should recall Churchill's assessment — 'a man of genius who might have become a man of destiny'.

The 1944 Japanese offensive, meanwhile, had erupted, first in the Arakan and then on the Central, Imphal, front. On 4 and 5 February a large force infiltrated through the eastern sector of the British Arakan position, moved west across its rear to occupy the east-to-west Ngakyedauk Pass and, on the 7th, attacked the headquarters and administrative echelons of 7th Indian Infantry Division.

Gen Sir William Slim, commander of the recently formed Fourteenth Army, had already instructed that those faced with such a situation must stand fast, pin the enemy around the defences and enable them to be destroyed by other formations; in the meantime, with now almost complete air supremacy, air supply would be arranged. At 7th Division's HQ it fell to the CRA, Brig A. F. Hely, to hold off the Japanese with the

113
Maj-Gen Orde Wingate, with (left) his Chief-of-Staff Brig D. D. C. Tulloch (also a Gunner) in Assam prior to the second Chindit expedition.
IWM

114
Chindit stronghold 'Broadway' — detachment of 69 LAA Regiment digging a Bofors gun-pit, March 1944.
Mrs Tulloch

men of his own artillery HQ, to maintain radio communication with the artillery regiments and, at noon on the 7th, to transfer control to the CO of 24th LAA Regiment in the Administrative area. Thither the divisional commander, Maj-Gen F. W. Messervy, made his way with his staff.

This area, lying in open 'paddy' fields (rice fields) surrounded by jungle and Japanese but organised for all-round defence, was known as the Sinzweya Box. It was successfuly defended until 23 February when counter-offensives by 5th and 26th Divisions cleared the communications and killed or drove-off the remains of the infiltrating force. From within the Box, using his CRA's radio network. Gen Messervy commanded his division; the defence of the box was conducted by Brig Geoffrey Evans, who had come to the early aid of 7th Division with a Gurkha battalion and two squadrons of tanks. Besides these there were the HQ and two batteries of 24th LAA Regiment, a troop of the 8th (Belfast) HAA Regiment, a 5.5in battery of 6th Medium Regiment, two batteries of 24th Indian Mountain Regiment and a mortar battery of 139th Jungle Field Regiment.

Brig Hely, in the *RA Commemoration Book*, writes:
'Gunners soon showed their versatility. HQ 24th LAA Regiment became HQ 7th Indian Division. Gunner signallers and sets were soon working to all brigades and as our communications with outside regiments had never been broken we were in a comfortable position. Ammunition for the guns in the Box was there for the taking, since the corps ammunition dump was in the centre of the valley.

'Outside the Box 136th Field Regiment, under Geoff Armstrong, and Harry Hall's 139th Field Regiment were safely with 33 Brigade; 25th Mountain Regiment, under Lewis Pugh, were with 114 Brigade; and 7th Indian Field Regiment were rather isolated some distance away, while 24th Mountain Regiment, under Humphrey Hill, were on the Box perimeter. The first two regiments had tremendous tasks. Not only did they shoot for their own brigade, but also, turning their guns round, they shot day after day and night after night for the beleaguered Box. They were particularly useful for counter-battery tasks, of which there were many.

'The Japs soon consolidated their positions around the Box. They occupied the hill features and could look down at all the activities of the garrison. Battle took place daily for the immediate hills, and it was with great difficulty that these were held. Cole's LAA boys, moving their Bofors around, shot Japs off many hill positions over open sights and supported infantry counterattacks.

'Jack Thompson of 24th LAA, not caring for the role of a static infantry soldier, soon discovered some mortars in the corps dump. Collecting odd cooks and drivers, he manned these mortars and used them very effectively. The mortars of 139th Jungle Field Regiment were particularly useful in the many short-range concentrations which were called for day after day and for the harassing tasks which were put down nightly on Jap positions. Replenishment of ammunition was a constant difficulty for them and their excellent quartermaster, Wallace, who lost his life while escorting an ammunition party.

'As the days wore on 5th Indian Division struggled to open a way in over the Ngakyedauk Pass and the sound of their guns getting nearer was a great comfort to the garrison. 26th Division approaching from the north was somewhat of a problem. We had 5th Division's call-signs before the battle started, but we had no means of communicating with 26th Division, and because of this our troops were being shelled consistently by the mountain guns of 26th Division as they approached. John Frith from 136th Field Regiment volunteered to break through the Jap lines and make contact with 26th Division. This he successfully did, and coming up on his wireless set on a RA net provided the contact which we badly needed.

'The guns outside the Box had been well stocked with ammunition in preparation for a big battle which the Jap forestalled. Their many commitments, however, soon left them rather short, and although aircraft dropped a certain amount, it was hardly enough to keep them going. Jamie Haworth, who was assistant staff captain RA, volunteered to take out a convoy from the Box to the guns outside. He successfully and gallantly ran the gauntlet on three occasions with very few casualties to his team.

'An outstanding feature of the siege was the magnificent work of the RA signallers. Never once, from the moment the Jap attacked HQ 7th Indian Division, was communication lost between HQRA and the units of the divisional artillery. Night and day wireless sets were kept in operation and signals were passed to brigades and formations. The organisations of the Box and its support from outside by guns was only made possible by the superhuman efforts of the Gunner signallers, who never failed to keep contact. Time and again when life was made uncomfortable for the inhabitants of the Box by Jap guns outside our range, Gunner signals make it possible for us to call for badly needed counter-battery fire from guns situated outside.'

In the second week of March the main Japanese offensive developed against the Imphal Plain. IV Corps withdrew to the southern and western outskirts of that Plain and was reinforced from the Arakan by 5th Division. Other Japanese thrusts came farther north, resolving themselves into the savage and prolonged battle of Kohima.

The first stage of this battle, the 'siege', lasted from 5 to 20 April. Col Hugh Richards was placed in command of a scratch force assembled around the 1st Assam Regiment, 3rd Assam Rifles and later 4th Royal West Kents (Lt-Col H. J. Laverty). With this he maintained a footing on the Kohima ridge, against theoretically impossible odds, until relieved by 2nd Infantry Division. Important factors in this defence were Maj R. de C. Yeo and the 3.7in howitzers and gunners of Lt-Col R. H. M. Hill's 24th Mountain Regiment, Indian Artillery. Yeo organised four permanently-manned OPs, while the little 3.7s, crammed together in a defended 'box' two miles west of the ridge, maintained their high reputation for accurate and consistent fire. To quote from C. E. Lucas Phillips's *Springboard to Victory*:

Burma, the Central Front.

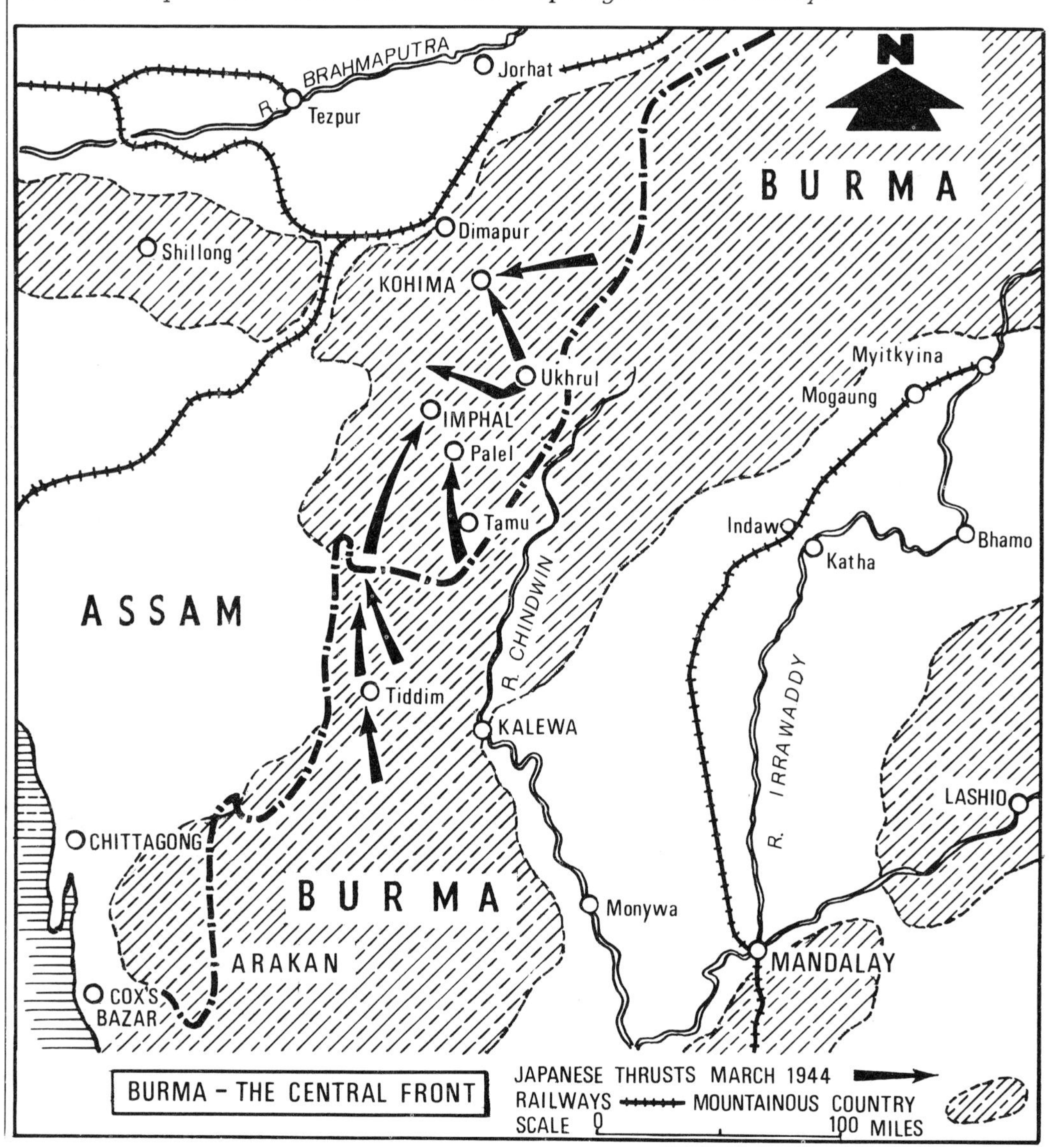

'Here the 3.7s very soon had the approaches to the Ridge "recorded" with absolute precision. Again and again they broke up enemy attacks just as they were being launched, by day and by night. Their response to an infantry demand for 'defensive fire' was swift and exact. The DFs that had soon to be fired on the tennis court were as close to the infantry as twenty yards. Not once during the whole siege did a shell land on the infantry within the perimeter, despite frequent switches and alterations of range at night. This was due, not only to good direction of fire, but also to what Hill himself called "the deadly accurate laying of our Indian gunners".

'At first Yeo kept his OPs with the infantry companies, but very soon the company commanders themselves were able to order any DF they wanted and to adjust it, speaking by telephone or wireless to Laverty's command post alongside Yeo's main OP.

'Nor was this all. Before very long the ears of the gunner officers became so well attuned that they could tell from the Japanese noises just where and when assaults were to be made and were able to anticipate the infantry demands before they were made. On several occasions during a night Laverty would call:

' "Gunner, DF No.6", and receive the quiet reply:

' "It's on the way, sir."

'There can seldom, indeed, have been a better example of infantry-artillery co-operation. Thus, while it cannot be said that any one unit was the sole battle-winner at Kohima — for several were to play a vital part — it is none the less certain that 24th Mountain Regiment was one of them and that without them Kohima could never have been held.'

As the relieving 2nd Division came up the road from Dimapur, Yeo was also able to control the fire of their 25pdrs. From 20 April that division (of XXXIII Corps) took over and consolidated the Kohima defences and, until 2 June when the Japanese finally withdrew, carried out a long sequence of attacks which, at great cost in casualties, finally gained full control of Kohima ridge, the high ground to north and south and the ability to move along the road towards Imphal.

The conditions in which Infantry and Gunners lived and fought this battle are not easy to describe, but the following extracts of a letter from Lt P. A. Densham to his parents, published in *Tales of the Mountain Gunners* (MacFetridge and Warren), go some way to doing so. Densham arrived to join 24th Mountain Regiment some ten days before the end of this long battle and, shortly after his arrival, was called up to an OP in 'Naga Village' — a devastated point of vantage (north of the main Kohima ridge) which was shared at that time between the 4th/15th Punjabs and the Japanese.

'On my third morning', he wrote, 'the CO called me up to his OP to take over from Richards. I reported at about 1900, feeling completely useless and very uneasy. The CO had John Nettlefield with him as aide. He turned to me and said "Have you ever seen a Jap?" Hearing that I hadn't he told John to show me some and then put me in the OP. There had been an attack the night before by the Japs, and two of them were lying dead only five yards from our forward posts. I said to John, "How disgusting". He said in genuine astonishment, "What, those? You will soon get to like them like that". He took me on a tour of inspection. Such

116
Kohima, Church Knoll from Naga Village. *IWM*

squalor and dirt I had never seen. Sheets of corrugated iron, old shell cases, tin cans and rubbish. The platoon up there were all living in holes in the ground. They seemed remarkably cheerful, smoking, or eating out of their mess-tins. I went forward and was told to keep my head down, which I did very thoroughly though I noticed that the Indian soldiers were wandering about quite unconcerned. The OP was very small, and we had to crawl in. It had a roof of tin and earth, and walls of stones. In front there were two loop-holes over-looking a small hill about 400 yards away. Between our hill and this other, which was called Church Knoll, were 400 yards of indescribable chaos.

'John said, "That's where the Jap is". I was horrified. It seemed terribly close, within rifle range. The Knoll was bare of everything except twisted stumps and ploughed blackish earth, with a crest only 100 yards long, rather like a big sand castle. There were 3 bunkers in the forward face, and several previous attacks on it had been unsuccessful. I took over from Richards, who looked yellowish and scruffy and said, "It's all yours. You're welcome to it". I sat on a sack beside my signaller who had a telephone and a wireless set. I watched the Knoll and saw nothing. Every now and then our shells would come over and crump down on it — harassing fire. I was told that there was to be another attack on it tomorrow and that we were to start softening it today.'

On the following day Densham went forward as FOO to D Company of the Punjabs:
'I met D Company Commander, a colossal man weighing 16 stone and a great cricketer. I felt great confidence in him, and he seemed quite cool and calm. There was a lot of laughter and joking, quite genuine and not of the film variety. Not knowing anyone, I sat quiet and listened. At last someone said, "We had better be getting along", and we filed out to put on tin hats and equipment. The start line for the attack was a nullah near my OP, well out of sight of the enemy, and here the two companies were formed up, waiting listlessly for zero hour. The Sikhs were going to the right and Mussulmans to the left of the objective. BORs usually talk on these occasions, but the Indians don't, and they squatted on their haunches, looking straight in front of them. Officers kept looking at their watches, and soon the artillery barrage started. The shells streamed overhead continuously for half an hour; the noise was stupefying and I could hardly think. I leaned against a rock and looked at my map, though it meant nothing and may have been upside down. The Sikhs got to their feet and began filing down the nullah. Each had one grenade ready, and another hooked into the belt by the lever. They went in first, running across the broken ground towards the hill. Our guns stopped, and there was complete silence. We could see them scrambling up the loose earth towards the top, and someone said, "They've done it! Well done, A Company!" Just then the Jap opened up his guns. He had kept them quiet for days, and I certainly didn't know he had any. The shells landed slap in the company, and many Sikhs scrambled back, while others lay where they were. A few went on to the top, and were met with hand grenades from the Japs entrenched just over the crest.

'Then D Company went in. I had no feelings at all. We went down the nullah and out into the open, while the wounded were being brought back. I thought we would be sniped, but nothing happened. All was as quiet as it had been before A Company went in. I found the Company Commander lying in a shallow depression at the bottom of the hill. He said, "I can't get my men to go in. Can you get your guns on to the top and try to keep the Jap's head down?" I got orders through and heard the shells going over. Suddenly there was a dull clang in my head and every-thing went black and far away. When I came to I found my signaller dead; he was sitting beside me, about two feet away. The Company Commander said, "Sorry about that, Gunner; he's mortaring us, I'm afraid". There was another dull clang, and I fell forward, resting my tin hat on the ground in front. I felt warm and tired, and nothing seemed to matter. I heard myself breathing a long way away. My head was so heavy that I could hardly lift it but managed it at last. The wireless was smashed, my other signaller had gone back wounded, not badly, and the Company Commander was unconscious and bleeding from his head. All the men had withdrawn and we were alone. I tried to pull him but could hardly move his arms. I went back and found some of his men and got them to come forward with me to help. We dragged him along the ground and got him on to a stretcher. I heard that he died four hours later. I went back to the nullah and found everyone very upset. The attack had been a complete failure and we had had nearly 100 casualties. I sat there feeling rotten. I was covered with blood, and soaked to the skin with sweat. I told the CO about the Company Commander, and that the remains of the Company were sheltering behind a wall and quite immovable. The 2nd-in-command asked me to show him where, and I went out again with him. We were sniped as soon as we had left cover, and I flattened down behind a few stones. A bullet smacked into the ground about a foot from my face. I didn't know what to do, so lay still. Then another came too close, and I realised that I was the target and wriggled back behind a rock. I lay there for about three minutes and then made a dash for it.

'The rest of the day was grim. In the afternoon poor old D Company was sent in again. "Absolute suicide", as the new very young Company Commander said. We went round to the flank this time and got to the bottom of the hill without opposition. A few mortar bombs fell near, but the Jap could not see us as we were in a ditch. The men couldn't be got to attack again; they just sat on the ground, not looking or thinking about anything. This sounds very terrible but I am told it is what happens when a unit has been kept in too long, and sometimes it has to be done. In the end three officers and three men went to the top where they were again grenaded. The Company Commander was missing, and with what I thought was superb bravery the 2nd-in-command went up again and dragged him back. He also died later. We got back, and I prayed that there might be no more attacks that day. There was none; the battalion was in a bad way and could not do any more. The CO took compassion on me and sent me back to the battery. On the way down, to round off the day, my orderly and I were sniped on the road, and a signaller was hit in the foot. It had been a bad beginning, but at least I felt that my battle inoculation was complete and "positive"!'

OPs in the Burma theatre

Rather a different problem than in the Desert.
117
Arakan, a flash-spotter's OP. *IWM*
118
Immobility in a forward position — 2-Lt B. K. Mehta of 24 Indian Mountain Regiment observes fire upon a target 300 yards away. *IWM*

117

118

While the battle of Kohima was being fought, IV Corps was engaged in almost as desperate, and certainly more widespread, defence of the Imphal Plain. Maj Warren Bugler was an OP officer and later Battery Commander in 114th Field Regiment, a Territorial Army unit of exceptional quality, formed in Sussex on the eve of war and from 1942 to 1945 part of the 20th Indian Infantry Division's artillery. Of the Imphal battle Bugler writes:

'The artillery observation posts were within infantry positions on hill features, mostly well dug in and encircled with wire. All that could usually be seen of the Japanese, except during an attack, was the blade of a shovel throwing up soil as trenches were made even deeper ... OPs were kept busy registering likely points of attack during the day, so that immediate fire could be brought down when the enemy was heard assembling or moving up for his inevitable night attack. Here the nature of the country made gunnery difficult, for example, an infantry patrol would report finding signs of Japs at cross tracks — a likely forming-up area — but these would not be marked on any available map nor could they be seen from the OP because of the trees, so that the wretched OP officer would be told "we want you to register cross tracks which are probably under the tallest of the trees you can see beyond that rock outcrop!"

'Every scrap of information was vital and OPs passed along most unlikely happenings in the hope that Divisional HQ could build up a complete picture. One report from my OP on East Crete only said "unusually tall Japanese seen wearing long white pullovers", but it was sufficient to tell the Intelligence Officers that the crack Japanese 33rd Division had been brought to this theatre from Korea. On another occasion, although we were accustomed to hearing "owls" hooting and other weird Japanese signalling noises all around us, I called up my brother Frank and asked him if he had heard English-sounding cuckoos just before dawn. He replied that there were indeed cuckoos in India but he had never heard one in Assam. My infantry commander ordered a "stand-to" and within minutes the Jap attack came in.'

On 10 April 1944 Signallers Doug Hawthorn and Les Duffin, also of 114,

close friends who had trained together, moved into an OP on Morgan's Peak, one of four notorious hills south of the Imphal Plain. Hawthorn tells the tale:

'As we gathered our equipment together Les seemed more subdued than usual and I have often wondered since whether he had some premonition of what was about to happen. The OP was frequently shelled and an attack on the position was always likely. About 4.30pm Les took his stint on the phone in our bunker and we sat talking and smoking. It would be dark by about 6 and as there could be no question of a fire after dark I went outside to scratch about for a few sticks to get a brew going. We lived pretty primitively in OP parties, especially when attached to Indian units when we survived on basic rations with bully and biscuits (all supplied by air drop) and very limited water supplies. Tea, the great reviver, and cigarettes to dull the appetite, were the mainstays.

'Hearing the Jap guns open up and the whine of the approaching shells I realised instinctively that I would never make it to our bunker and threw myself flat. Our "home" had received a direct hit, I was just showered with dirt and gravel, Les was lying wounded and clearly beyond help. I gave him our emergency morphia and he died with the shelling continuing. The OP officer, Captain Collin, took stock of the situation; the phone and the radios were smashed but I established lamp communication with the guns whilst our gallant Indian companions held off the infantry attack to which the shelling was the prelude. My lamp shone out like a searchlight in the darkness but the 25-pounders responded magnificently, the shells crashing down on the slopes and fully playing their part in beating off the attack, leaving me with my memories and the sickening stench of death.'

Maj-Gen Geoffrey Collin, as he became, later wrote of this episode:
'Although we had to rely entirely on the use of our lamp, each time its beam pierced the night it was greeted with a hail of bullets and mortar fire and Signaller Hawthorn had to transmit for a minute — duck back into the trench and after a brief pause pop out some feet away and send another brief series. We opened fire on hearing the unmistakable sound of the Japs forming up in the jungle some 150

yards away; our first shells landed well away from the target, we anxiously gave corrections based on our estimate by sound only of where they landed. Soon the shells were landing outside our own wire and by the cries and evident confusion they were breaking up the Jap attack. At least four further attacks during the night were disrupted by shell fire, together with grim and close-quarter fighting by our companions. Once again I experienced that tremendous bond of respect and confidence that existed between all our OP parties and the infantry with whom they lived and fought.'

By the end of June the Japanese were retreating. They were not routed, however, and at every stage IV and XXXIII Corps needed to overcome stubborn resistance. The Gunners had also to overcome severe natural obstacles, not only to move forward with their infantry but also to coax their guns into positions among the mountains and jungle from which they could bring down fire where the infantry needed it. The advance was slow, therefore, and it was not until December 1944 that the two Corps started to cross the River Chindwin. By then 36th Division, which had relieved the Chindits in North Burma, had advanced south to the Indaw area.

Early in December an advance was made in the Arakan, once again towards Akyab. Characteristically this inspired aggressive Japanese moves to the east of it, against 81st West African Division in the Kaladan valley. Generally these attacks were well contained but, in the area of Tinma, 30

119
Shenam, south of Imphal, April 1944. Sgt Frank Bostock and 3.7in howitzer of 232 Battery, 114 Field Regiment. Unopened bully-beef tins were used to reinforce the gun platform, but subsequently had to be dug-up and their contents devoured.
Warren Bugler

120
On leave in Calcutta, October 1944, Douglas Hawthorne (left) and Ken Gwynne, both of 114 Field Regiment.
Douglas Hawthorne

Advance on the Arakan front, December 1944

121
25pdr and Jeep of 27 Field Regiment afloat down the Kalapanzin River. *IWM*

122
27 Regiment's OP party on the move. *IWM*

123
30 Indian Mountain Regiment crossing a chaung. *IWM*

124
Havildar Umrao Singh VC, of 30 Regiment.
Royal Artillery Charitable - Fund

miles east of Buthidaung, a 3.7in howitzer section of 30th Indian Mountain Regiment was isolated in a forward position, subjected to prolonged artillery and mortar fire and then to a series of night attacks by infantry which finally overran the section.

Six hours later counter-attacks recovered the section position. One man was found alive, Havildar Umrao Singh, No 1 of one of the gun detachments; he was found lying beside his own gun with severe wounds. In the final hand-to-hand fighting he had wielded with deadly effect the 'gun bearer', a metal shaft used to support the rear end of the 3.7in 'piece' when assembling and dismantling. Around him lay 10 dead Japanese.

Havildar Umrao Singh had saved his gun, which fired again that day. He survived to receive the Victoria Cross.

8 Into Europe

After the long North African campaign the next step was the invasion of southern Europe. On the night of 9 July 1943 the British Eighth Army landed at the south-east corner of Sicily against little opposition. The American Seventh Army landed to the west of it and drove across the island to Palermo. Both armies then converged upon Messina, immediately opposite the 'toe' of Italy; German resistance was stiff during the latter part of the campaign but by 16 August Messina had fallen and the German army had crossed to the mainland.

Initially the enemy had air superiority and the Allied AA Gunners, therefore, were correspondingly busy. Lt-Col G. L. Moss, who had much experience of LAA units and operations, has left an unpublished manuscript in which he has explained with clarity their special problems:

'The range of a Bofors gun is very limited, something under two thousand yards, so whatever shooting could be done had to be done in a very few seconds. An approaching target at 2000 feet comes into range for perhaps two or three seconds — not much time for a gun crew to get ready and to shoot it down. For this very reason a gun team has always to be on its toes and must be ready for action throughout daylight at ten seconds notice. When this is realised it will be seen that at least three men of a gun crew of seven had to be always and constantly on the watch and Heaven help them if an enemy plane came over flying low and it was not shot-at.'

The difficulty of actually scoring a lethal hit during the available two or three seconds can readily be imagined. Even if such hit was scored, the aircraft might not crash for seconds or even minutes after the hit, in which case its destruction might not become common knowledge nor be 'credited' to the unit concerned. A Bofors detach-ment, however, will have performed much of its task if it forced the aircraft's pilot to take evasive action and thus dispense with accurate bombing or cannon fire. It will have further performed its task if it discouraged pilots from pressing-home future attacks in that area. In the Eighth Army's advance from El Alamein to Tunis 2nd LAA Regiment, of which Moss was 2nd-in-command, had the role of protecting the advanced landing-grounds of the Desert Air Force; Moss remarks: 'From Alamein to Tunis the RAF did not lose one single aircraft from enemy ground attacks from the air. Surely a great triumph for the AA defences?'

In Sicily Moss commanded 18th LAA Regiment. His troops landed on the beaches with the leading brigades and claimed their first victim within minutes of landing. In the first eight days his regiment was credited with 28 enemy aircraft. Moss describes an engagement, which he personally watched, on 17 July 1943, about 15 miles south of Catania on the east coast:

'At Lentini we had from our point of view the most successful engagement of the campaign. Two of our batteries and one of another LAA Regiment (in fact 25th LAA Regiment) were concentrated in the area... Nine 109s came over low and were met by a regular hail of LAA fire. In all we shot down (officially confirmed) five enemy aircraft and a further two, not confirmed, were seen to drop in the sea... I watched the whole show and I do not think I ever derived more pleasure from anything.'

The Sicilian campaign persuaded the Italians that for them the war was over. On 25 July Mussolini, 'Il Duce', resigned, the Italian King handed the government of the country to Marshal Badoglio and the latter opened negotiations with the Allies. Arguments as to

the precise meaning of 'unconditional surrender' wasted valuable time, however, while fresh German divisions (under Marshal Kesselring), poured over the Alps into Italy. Not until 3 September was the armistice signed; this delay made Italy a battleground.

On 3 September, also, the Eighth Army landed on the mainland of Italy, opposite Messina. A formidable concentration of artillery had been built-up on the west side of the straits, with spectacular observation, but there was little opposition when the straits were crossed. The Eighth Army quickly occupied Taranto and advanced northwards, a division along each coast. Meanwhile, early on 9 September, the American General Mark Clark's Fifth Army, which included the British X Corps, began to land on the west coast of Italy, at Salerno, some 30 miles south of Naples. By now the German Army and Air Force were in position to take a hand.

Brig F. S. Siggers, then CCRA X Corps, wrote, for the *RA Commemoration Book:*

'At 3.45 a.m on September 9th the leading craft began to touch-down; Gunner recce parties went in with their leading infantry, followed by the first 25-pr and anti-tank troops, amid the roar of bombardment from supporting ships and aircraft. By nightfall elements of some 13 regiments were ashore — but by no means without incident. 71st Field Regiment had a LST [Landing Ship, Tank] holed by shellfire just off the beaches, vehicles were engaged and set on fire by 88mm, and the leading troop had to fight its way into action against heavy machine-gun and mortar fire; but this did not prevent them from having guns in action two miles inland by the evening. 113th Field Regiment had a hard battle to get across the beaches into the close vineyards and tomato groves, harried continously by the elusive enemy snipers. 65th Field Regiment, too, were not to miss their share of adventure. Some vehicles and guns landed in soft sand and one landing craft stuck off shore. But strenuous man-handling solved these difficulties — sharpened up wonderfully by the bark of the hostile Bredas and the thump of mortars. But we suffered a very grievous loss at the time in the sinking of a LCT [Landing Craft, Tank] with her precious SP Troop of the Devon Yeomanry, which was going in with 64th Field Regiment.'

125
Avola, Sicily, July 1943, Bofors of 327 Battery, 99 LAA Regiment. *IWM*

126
Near Catania, Sicily, July 1943, 4.5in detachment of 227 Medium Battery snatch a quick lunch. *IWM*

127
Sicily and Italy 1943-45.

The air defence of the beaches was vital; an AA group, under Lt-Col G. V. M. Chadd, landed early on D day. Chadd's report on the landings (Royal Artillery Institution Military Document MD/419) has as an appendix a very articulate report by his driver-batman, Gnr J. Lester, who accompanied D Troop, 328th LAA Battery, and a battalion of the Hampshire Regiment, in an LST.

At 3.15am the Hampshires began to embark in assault-craft, upon which enemy shelling also began and caused casualties. About three hours later, as planned, the LST touched-down but was waved-off because fighting was still taking place on the beach and the LST was attracting 88mm gunfire. At 12.30pm they tried again but were again waved-off. At 2.30 they came in for the third time, grounded and lowered the ramp. Gnr Lester, with No 1 Gun, continues:

'As the ramp went down the LAA gunners were told to make a bolt for it with their guns. I was with the leading gun which was being towed by a four-by-four 3-ton vehicle loaded with ammunition. The vehicle and gun both cleared the ramp but the 3-tonner left the wire track about 15 yards up the

The Salerno landing

128
Quad and 25pdr drive away
from the water's edge. *IWM*
129
Bishop of 142 Field Regiment
— one of the first guns
ashore. *IWM*
130
Bofors detachment of 122
Battery, 13 LAA Regiment, in
Salerno Bay. *J. Johnson*
131
German Mark IV Specials
destroyed by 231 Battery, 58
Anti-tank Regiment. *IWM*

129

beach, digging its wheels into the sand. In the meantime the 88-mm guns had again opened up and it was obvious that the LST would be sunk if she stayed where she was. An AMLO ('Assistant Military Landing Officer') ordered the ship away, leaving the Bofors gun and towing vehicles with the detachment to do the best they could.

'The assistance of a bulldozer was obtained and after an extremely uncomfortable 20 minutes we managed to get the gun on to hard ground about 100 yards from the water's edge, where the Detachment Commander (No 1) gave orders for it to be put into action. I assisted with the unloading of ammunition. Before the gun was in action we were engaged at close range by mortar fire from inland.

130

131

'Once into action Nos 2 and 3 remained on the gun and the rest of us took cover in a ditch. After about half an hour we dug slit trenches near the gun, into which we climbed. One man received a serious splinter-wound in the face from an 88-mm shell. The infantry did not seem to have advanced more than about 200 to 300 yards from where we were, and all the officers had been killed, in addition to hundreds of other ranks.

'At about 1800 hours the mortars quietened down and an officer came along and explained that an attack was expected at dusk and if it came there would be insufficient material on Green Beach to withstand it, but that a pincer movement by our troops from adjoining beaches was to be attempted. No attack materialised but constant rifle, machine gun, bren and mortar fire was heard throughout the night. By daylight all was reasonably quiet and LSTs began to unload on the beach without interruption. The 88-mm battery on our right flank had been silenced.

'In my opinion the No 1 of the gun behaved magnificently the whole time, and was the first man to contact his battery on Red Beach on the morning after we landed. I found the whole experience extremely frightening, but once we had got our gun into action the whole detachment seemed to gain confidence and did not care very much what happened.'

By the morning of the 10th the bridgehead could be considered established. Hard battles had to be fought both to the south and north and Gunner OPs, in particular, paid a heavy price. But on the 16th contact was made with Eighth Army patrols advancing up the west coast, by the 23rd the bridgehead was expanding, eight days more and Naples was occupied.

The battle-line moved north, with torrential rain and mud inhibiting mobility. Lance-Bombardier Spike Milligan was there, in 19th Battery of 56th Heavy Regiment; the following extract from his *Mussolini, his part in my downfall* paints a convincing picture of an artillery specialist who is usually rather short of publicity — the linesman-signaller:

'Twas a dark and stormy night and the Monkey-truck signallers lay dead asleep. At the soul-shattering hour of 0100 hours, with a gale blowing and rain squalling the tempest-black night, a cry is hurled among the dormant bodies.

'"The OP line is dis"'

'Reacting like a Pavlov dog, Edgington rises, dons his boots, and plunges into the night. He follows the wire, falls into a three-foot muddy stream, mends the break. At dawn, while we were taking the first tea of the day, a spectre appears at the Command Post entrance, it is the same height as Edgington . . . it *is* Edgington, from head to foot it drips with water and mud overlaid with a fine layer of frost. Two eyes look out from the mud. It groans.'

Eighth Army, on the east side of the central hills, occupied the important Foggia group of airfields on 27 September and by 9 November had reached the Sangro river, 150 miles north of Taranto. There the Germans were well entrenched and heavy rain and floods deferred the assault until 28 November. Success in this battle depended particularly on firepower. By this time

132
3.7in HAA gun firing in the ground role, November 1943. For the rest of the war the use of HAA batteries in the long-range field artillery role became quite frequent. *IWM*

133
Sangro River battle, November 1943. Linesmen-signallers of 132 Field Regiment approaching an OP with caution. *IWM*

it had become the practice to concentrate heavy and medium artillery (usually with some field guns) into artillery formations known as 'Army Groups, Royal Artillery', referred to always as 'Agras'. 1st and 6th Agra supported Eighth Army on the Sangro, comprising altogether one heavy, seven medium and two field regiments. Observation of the fire of so many long-range guns was a problem, the solution of which was assisted by 651 Air OP Squadron (which had landed with Eighth Army in the toe of Italy) but also by the revival in this battle of the art of Air Force-Artillery cooperation.

The art seemed to have died out with the Lysander in Libya in 1941, but had been kept alive in the training echelons and adapted to speech-radio and to the Uncle-Target procedure. In Tunisia, in 1943, No 40 Squadron, South African Air Force, a famous reconnaissance squadron, had made attempts at 'artillery co-op' which were, however, frustrated by radio difficulties. In Sicily and southern Italy their CO, Lt-Col W. A. Nel, determined to make a success of it, practised the art first with the Royal Navy and then with the Eighth Army artillery. In the

Sangro battle, now flying Spitfires, the pilots of No 40 Squadron flew large numbers of artillery sorties against the hostile artillery, and achieved excellent results. Three RAF squadrons (Nos 208, 225 and 318 (Polish)) enthusiastically and effectively adopted this role, very well suited to the many deliberate Allied attacks on fortified areas or across river lines, which became a feature of the Italian campaign.

On the west side of Italy the Fifth Army came up against the German Gustav line based on the Rapido River and Monte Cassino. In January 1944 an attempt was made to outflank this line by a seaborne landing in the Anzio peninsula, 40 miles south of Rome, by the United States VI Corps, including 1st British Infantry Division and later another such division. The landing was virtually unopposed but progress thereafter was slower than had been hoped; the Germans rapidly concentrated around the beachhead and, throughout the month of February, attacked with great violence. The beachhead shrunk to a triangle of ground 13 miles at its greatest width and seven miles deep. In the British sector were concentrated some four hundred guns, medium, field, anti-tank and light anti-aircraft, together with two Air OP Flights of No 655 Squadron.

Brig J. M. S. Pasley was CRA, 1st Division, and senior British Gunner in the beachhead. Of this period of the battle he writes, in the *RA Commemoration Book:*

'It was during this "touch-and-go" period that comradeship between British and Americans and between Gunners and their infantry and armour reached a pitch never surpassed, and perhaps never equalled, in the whole course of the war. Their confidence and trust in one another were superb and always superbly justified. The infantry lived in a continuous atmosphere of murderous battle of an intensity they had never imagined. They fought until it was impossible to go on; and then went on. In three weeks they averaged over 500 casualties per battalion. They were in sore need of something to depend on, something to lean against. They found that "something" in their Gunners. Every brigade commander swore that his Gunners were unique. Here is part of a letter from one of these commanders to his Field Regiment:

' "I can assure you that no brigade has ever been so magnificently 'looked after' (and I use that term in its full sense of intimate help and co-operation) as this brigade has been by your grand Field Regiment. Throughout the Brigade, the feeling of confidence and trust in your Regiment is quite phenomenal, and, of course, entirely due to the results your Regiment has produced. I should be most grateful if you would convey these remarks to all ranks of the Regiment."

'Some idea of the intensity of the fighting may be gained when it is realised that in the course of these three weeks, in the augmented artillery of 1st Division alone:

'There were over 600 casualties, including 50 officers.

'19 gunpits suffered direct hits from shellfire or bombing.

'50 OP wireless sets were destroyed, either by enemy action or deliberately to avoid capture.

'24 anti-tank guns were overrun and lost.

'19th Field Regiment lost, in three days, their commanding officer, their second-in-command, and two of the three battery commanders.

'Just under 500,000 rounds were fired. (One gun of 78th Field Regiment fired 706 rounds in 24 hours.)

'111th Battery of 80th (Scottish Horse) Medium Regiment moved five miles by night, fired 2,174 rounds from the new position, and brought 3,742 rounds either from the old position or from an equally distant dump. Each man handled three tons.'

The area of the beachhead was flat and good OP positions were in short supply. The need for Air OPs was correspondingly greater and in this battle all lingering doubts about the Air OP concept finally disappeared. It so happened that several members of 80th (Scottish Horse) Medium Regiment had been accepted for training as Air OP pilots and now found themselves in one or other Air OP flight at Anzio, alongside their parent regiment. Sgt B. C. Gluning was one of these, and in an article in the *Journal of Army Aviation* of 1973 described a typical 'fire-orders radio' exchange of the beachhead:

'(*Air OP) Pilot:* "Hello Peter Six, Mike Target, Mike Target, Mike Target (a Regimental target). Two hundred enemy forming up. Fire by order, Scale twelve, report when ready, over."

'*CRA 1 Div (Brig. Pasley) — interrupting:* "Big Sunray here. Cancel last order Peter Six, give him Victor Target (Corps Artillery), scale twelve. Fire by order, report when ready to Peter Six. Carry on Peter Six, well done, Out."

'The fire brought down would be from 124 25-prs, 24 Medium and 24 Heavies.'

Operating within enemy artillery range, vulnerable to low-level enemy fighter sweeps, their sorties carried out amid streams of shells from their own artillery, Air OP casualties had to be expected. Two pilots were shot down and killed, three more hit by their own shells, of whom one pilot died. Close liaison betwen field and AA units and their Air OP pilots prevented much greater casualties.

The Anzio garrison, British and American, weathered the storm. 'The last days of February', wrote Pasley, 'produced a feeling that Kesselring had shot his bolt.'

The Gustav Line, meanwhile, was still intact and held by the German Tenth Army. Attempts to break the defences were mostly directed at the eastern end, and particularly at Cassino and Monte Cassino. Bombing

Anzio Beachhead, January to June 1944

134
Priest of 22 Battery, 24 Field Regiment, coming ashore.
IWM

135
5.5in gun of 80 Medium Regiment (Scottish Horse).
IWM

136
February, 78 Field Regiment, Lance-Bombardier S. Williams in the wireless trench.   *IWM*

137
February, 655 Air OP Squadron, Auster approaching to land.   *IWM*

138
Capt Sandy Gordon, Air OP commander in the beachhead — painting by Capt J. J. Standfield on a farmhouse wall.   *IWM*

139
February, Bofors detachment of 313 Battery, 90 LAA Regiment, having just shot down an enemy aircraft.
IWM

138

139

140

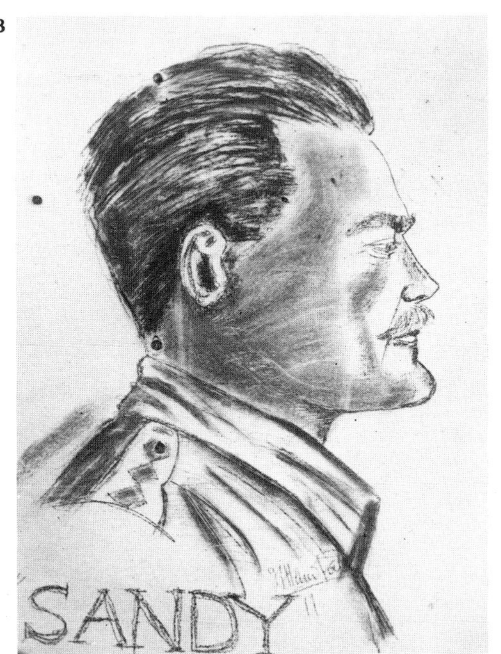

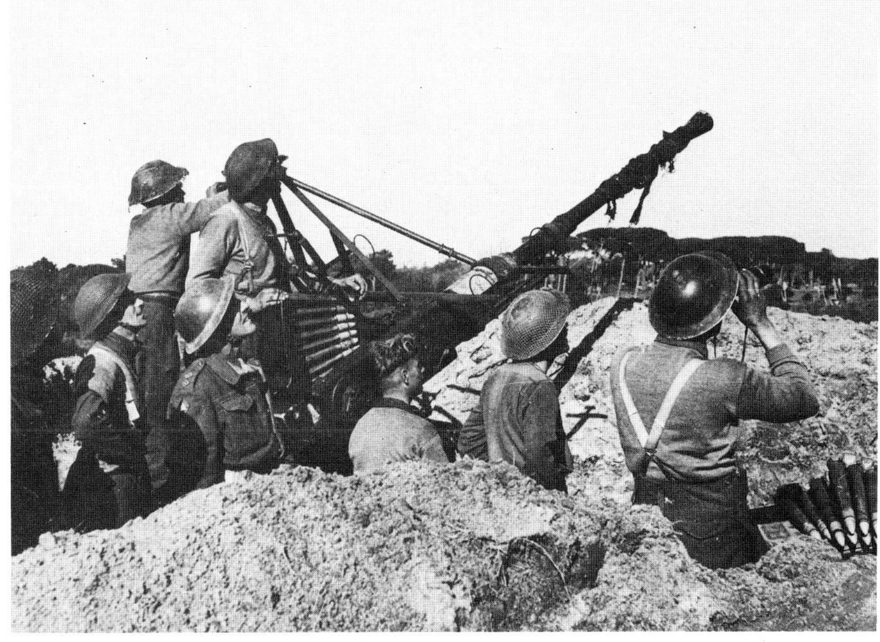

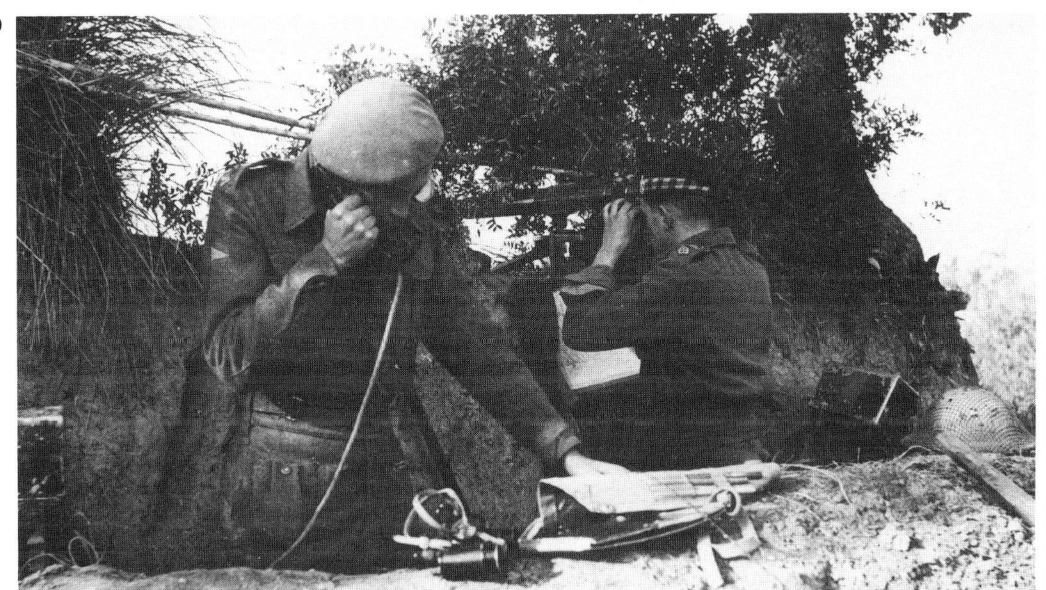

OPs in Italy

140
Sangro River, November 1943. Lt J. C. Thomas, 80 Medium Regiment (Scottish Horse), observing. *IWM*

141
Auster III taking-off in the Sangro area. *IWM*

142
Spitfire V, with which the art of 'Artillery Reconnaissance' was revived. *IWM*

143
Lt-Col W. A. Nel, OC 40 Squadron, South African Air Force, the tall officer towards the left of the group, alongside George and Beryl Formby. Nel took the initiative with artillery reconnaissance and his example spread. *South African National Museum of Military History*

141

142

143

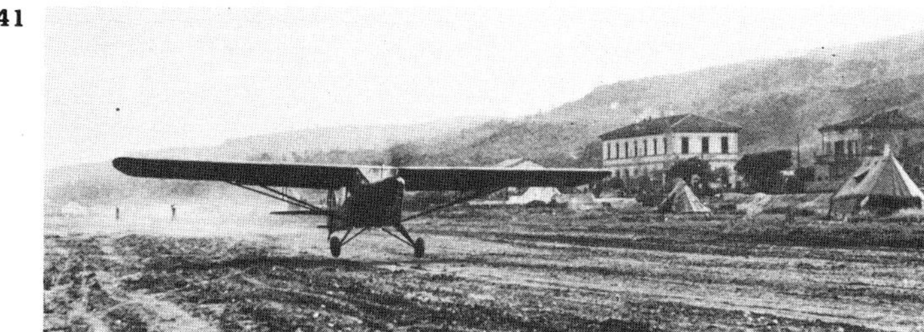

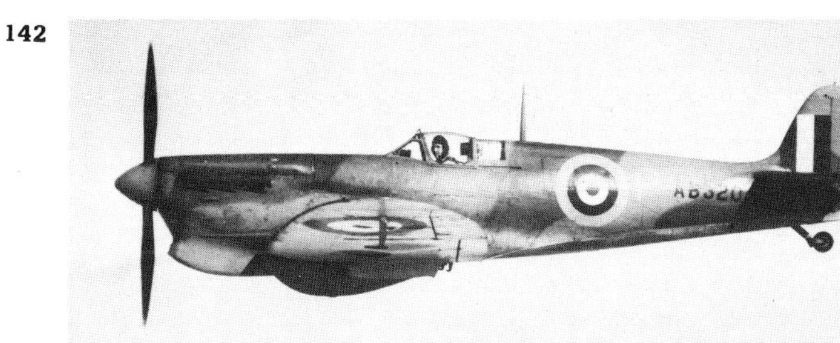

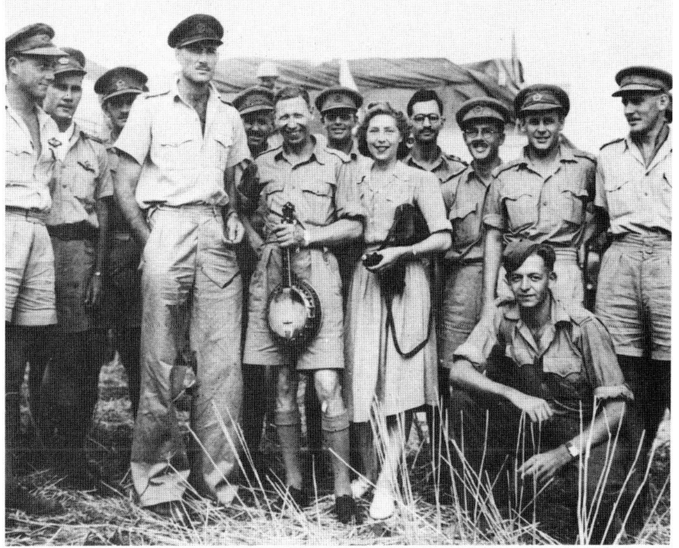

144
Gustav Line-Rapido River sector. 25pdr of 152 Field Regiment (Ayrshire Yeomanry) in action. *IWM*

Flash-spotting

A method of locating enemy artillery — 55 Observation Battery.
145
OP, where the compass-bearing of an enemy gun-flash was recorded and passed to the troop plotting centre. *IWM*
146
On the quadrant board strings from the plotted positions of several OPs were stretched out at the bearings reported from each. Point of intersection indicated the enemy gun position. *IWM*

145

146

and artillery concentrations on an enormous scale left Monte Cassino as difficult an infantry objective and as profitable an enemy OP area as at the start of the fighting.

In May the final attack was made by the Eighth and Fifth armies together, the former attacking across the Rapido and up the Liri valley, west of Cassino, while the Fifth Army advanced in the hilly coastal sector. The Eighth Army deployed more than a thousand guns, many of them long-range medium or heavy guns engaging the German artillery. Three air force squadrons, Nos 40, 208 and 225, were employed primarily in observing this 'counter-battery' fire.

As the German Tenth Army withdrew from the Gustav Line to an Adolph Hitler Line up the Liri valley, a British artillery record was established. On 23 May Brig Ziegler, CRA 1st Canadian Division, called for a 'William Target' against German infantry and tanks assembling for a counter-attack. This was a call for the whole of the Eighth Army artillery; 33 minutes later more than 600 guns opened-up together and in the next two minutes 3,500 shells descended on the target.

As the Tenth Army withdrew again the American divisions on the south flank of the Anzio beachhead broke out on to the flank of the German withdrawal. There seemed more than a chance of destroying this German army, but the eye of Gen Mark Clark would seem to have been rather on Rome, which, after severe fighting on the approaches, his Fifth Army entered on 4 June 1944.

Two days later the Allied descent on

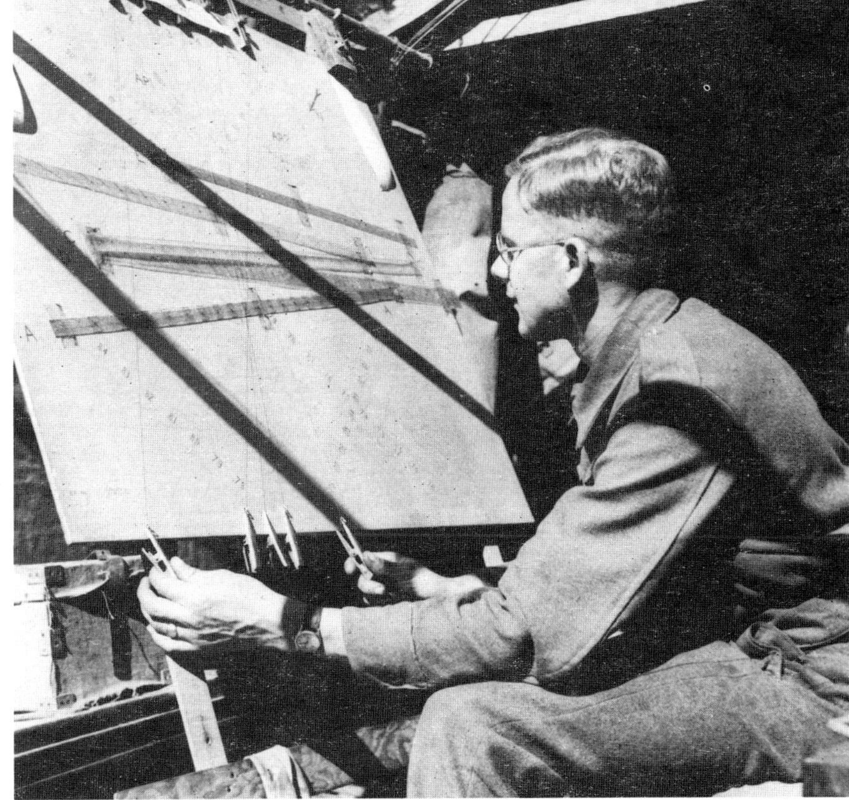

Sound-ranging

Another method of enemy gun location — 56 Observation Battery.

147
One of several microphones placed on a sound-ranging 'base'. They activated recorders at Sound-ranging HQ which produced a film-record of the timing of gun-firings 'heard' by each microphone. *IWM*

148
The directions and timings of gun-firings 'heard' by several microphones enabled plots to be made on a board, where intersections of plots indicated enemy gun positions. *IWM*

149
East of Rome, June 1944, 25pdr of 160 Battery, 57 Field Regiment, in action among the harvesters. *IWM*

150
August 1944, Florence area. Manhandling a 5.5in gun of 78 Medium Regiment round a bend of a mountain road. *IWM*

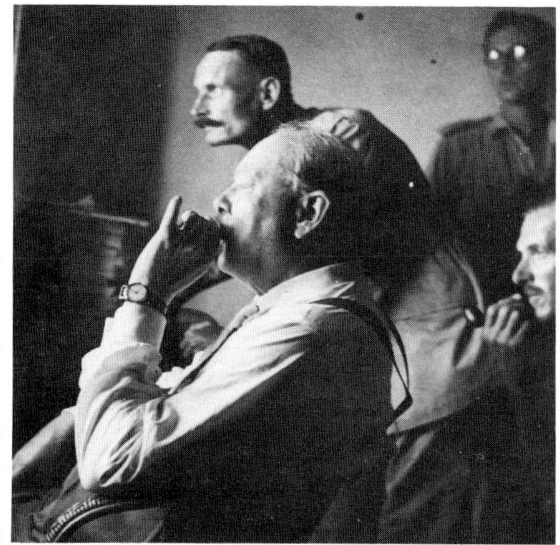

151
In an OP south of the River Arno, August 1944, Winston Churchill, Brig J. St C. Holbrook, Commander 6 AGRA and (right below) Lt-Col H. S. Thuillier, CO 66 (Lowland) Medium Regiment. Churchill was informed that 100 guns were concentrated on a particular target, ready to fire at his word. 'Churchill', wrote Thuillier in *Gunner* of July 1979, 'took off his jacket, rolled up his sleeves, lit a large cigar and said, "Now, this is just like sending a rude postcard and being there when it arrives. Fire!" '. *IWM*

Normandy took place. From then onwards the Italian operations had lower priority for both sides; furthermore the Allied forces there were 'milked' to provide for the invasion of the south of France in August and later for operations in Greece. Pressure was however maintained on Kesselring's army as it withdrew. The latter stood on another well-prepared position, the Gothic Line, extending across Italy from Spezia to Pesaro, and withdrew in September after a month of the bloodiest fighting in Italy. The end of the year found the Germans on the line of the Senio river, north of Ravenna, and in the north-east Appenines.

152
93 Battery, 70 Medium Regiment, September 1944 — 'Premature' in 5.5in gun, fortunately without casualties. *J. A. Holt*

153
Artificial Moonlight, to assist night operations, by 323 Searchlight Battery south-east of Bologna, December 1944. *IWM*

154
Winter in the Appenines. 461 Battery of 85 Mountain Regiment (75mm guns) receives ammunition by mule train. *IWM*

9 Beginning of the End

Among the many steps taken after Dunkirk to provide for the defence of the realm, not the least important were measures taken to carry out raids upon the coasts of enemy-occupied territory. These maintained an offensive spirit in a generally defensive environment, gave encouragement to the people of the occupied countries and enforced upon the enemy defensive measures which immobilised military manpower.

The attack on Dieppe by the 2nd Canadian Division on 19 August 1942, however, was a reconnaissance in force, a 'trial-run' for the invasion almost two years later. The assaulting units never gained a firm foothold and withdrew with severe casualties. An associated operation west of the town, carried out by No 4 Commando, to neutralise a German 155mm battery, was successful, and Maj Patrick Porteous, liaison officer between two detachments directed at separate points in the defences, became the third British Gunner of World War 2 to win the Victoria Cross. His citation stated:

'In the initial assault Major Porteous, working with the smaller of the two detachments, was shot at close range through the hand, the bullet passing through the palm and entering his upper arm. Undaunted, Major Porteous closed with his assailant, succeeded in disarming him, and killed him with his own bayonet, thereby saving the life of a British sergeant on whom the German had turned his aim.

'In the meantime the larger detachment was held up, and the officer leading his detachment was killed and the troop sergeant major fell seriously wounded. Almost immediately afterwards the only other officer of the detachment was also killed.

'Major Porteous, without hesitation and in the face of withering fire, dashed across the open ground to take over command of this detachment. Rallying them, he led them in a charge which carried the German position at the point of the bayonet, and was severely wounded for the second time. Though shot through the thigh he continued to the final objective, where he eventually collapsed from loss of blood after the last of the guns had been destroyed.'

In the endless battle of AA and Fighter Commands against the Luftwaffe, the most important developments of 1943 and 1944 were those of Radar. It became, as we have seen, an accepted means not only of acquiring and following a target but also of transmitting the information regarding it which was needed at the guns. Since the future-position, not the present-position, of the target was what interested the gunlayers, however, the radar's information still needed to pass through the predictor. At radar and predictor and at the transmission dials and fuze-setting machines were human beings, all capable of small

155
Capt Patrick Porteous VC.
From a portrait in oils by A. E. Haswell Miller via Royal Artillery Institution

Radar SCR 584.
Royal Artillery Institution

inaccuracies and occasional errors which, together, made up a lack of consistency in target-engagement. From the United States, however, came hope of a new radar, the SCR584, which would 'lock-on to' a target, leaving the operator with the one function of 'following-for-range'. A new electronic predictor would not only retransmit automatically to the bearing, elevation and fuze-length dials of the 3.7in guns but actually apply power to set the gun to its predicted bearing and elevation, to set the fuzes on the shells and to load the latter. The radar sets which would set in train this formidable automatic sequence of events would be situated at the batteries, not at detached operation-rooms.

By the middle of 1943 there were only small quantities of these magic radars and predictors in Great Britain. Furthermore, for the full measure of automatic operation the static Mark IIC gun was required and needed to be emplaced on a concrete holdfast.

During 1943 it became apparent that the Germans were preparing to launch, from the Channel coast against the south-east England, a quantity of pilotless aircraft filled with explosive. The RAF carried out attacks on such launching-sites as were found and

Fighter and AA Commands prepared plans to defend London. Their plans incorporated a belt of balloons along the line of the North Downs and of guns immediately south of it, with fighters operating south of the gun area. Gen Sir Frederick Pile, of AA Command, sent a personal representative to America to express the urgency with which we required SCR584 Radars, No 10 Predictors and also the British-invented but American-produced VT fuzes. At the same time the Royal Electrical and Mechanical Engineers (REME) of AA Command developed a portable platform of railway rails, the Pile Platform, anchored upon which the 3.7in Mark IIC gun could dispense with a concrete holdfast.

The British started their return to northern Europe in the small hours of 6 June 1944, when 6th Airborne Division and two American airborne divisions landed behind the foremost enemy defences. 6th Division's role was to seize bridges over the River Orne (on the east flank of the planned beachhead) and the high ground beyond the river, and thus to protect the left flank of the main invasion force.

FOOs of 3rd Infantry Division and

Forward Observation Bombardment (FOB) parties were landed by parachute and glider to enable both army and naval artillery to support the airborne troops; anti-tank artillery, arriving by glider, was in action by 10am and by nightfall had a small bag of tanks to its credit. A battery of 53rd Worcestershire Yeomanry Light Regiment had also landed by glider and its 75mms were in action, and finally guns of 92nd and 93rd LAA Regiments, landed by sea, were in action around the Orne bridges.

From H-hour (7am) on D-day the main seaborne force was landing, the British 21st Army Group under Gen Montgomery on the east of the bridgehead, the American 12th Army Group under Gen Omar N. Bradley on the west, Montgomery acting as C-in-C until Eisenhower assumed control on 1 September.

Capt J. P. Cook was FOO of 90th (City of London) Field Regiment, RA, equipped with Sexton SP guns. With two signallers and an OPA he was to land at H+20 minutes, collecting his OP tank on the beach. He would call for fire from a Royal Marine battery manning Centaurs (Cromwell tanks carrying 95mm guns), from other SP guns firing from landing-craft, from two destroyers and from his own guns once they had landed at H+60 minutes. Cook and his party climbed into assault boats at 5.45am, in a choppy sea, and opened-up their radio. The flotilla formed up and headed for shore. Cook, in his account for the *RA Commemoration Book*, continues:

'Suddenly out of the smoke appeared the coast-line and the rocket ships steaming close inshore let their contribution go in two salvos. It didn't look as if much could survive at the wrong end of those rockets, if they were hitting their target. All very good for the morale of the spectators in the assault craft.

'Arromanches appeared unmistakably out of the smoke and we spotted that much-photographed landmark "The Wreck" lying on the beach to the west. We altered our course slightly and headed for a point some 400 yards to the west of the Wreck. The coast batteries had now woken up and some shells were bursting around us, but we were small, well-spaced and moving fast, and we felt pretty safe.

'We beached perfectly clearing all underwater obstacles, and paddled ashore in 18 inches of water. A fortunate start. The beach was being liberally swished with automatic fire from the right flank and we doubled smartly into a bomb hole, tore the waterproofing from our wireless sets and got rid of our life-belts. We called our armoured OP and the Centaurs repeatedly but got no answer from either. This was a blow, for we might

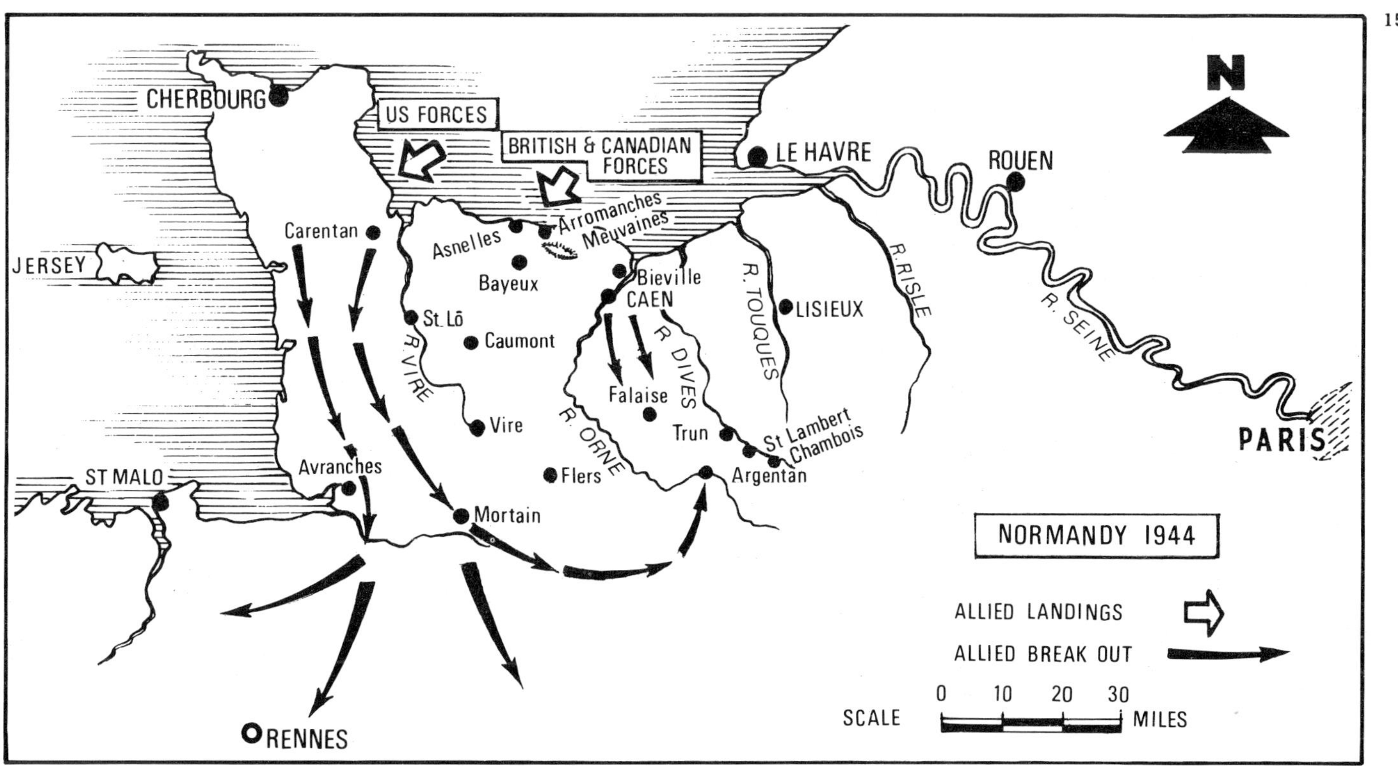

D-Day, 6 June 1944

158
On the beach. *IWM*
159
Priest SP 105mm guns of 33
Field Regiment early ashore.
IWM

want the latter at any moment now. We made a quick search for them on the beach without success. It wasn't too healthy a spot by this time, so we found C Company HQ and pushed across the sand dunes with them. We continued to call the Centaurs, but got no answering signal from them or the OP, and we feared the worst. We found out a few days later that their craft had shipped enough water to flood their engine-room and had drifted off the Isle of Wight for two days before being towed back to England.

'Troops were pretty thick on the beach by now and the small-arms fire from the right was doing some damage. Shells were bursting on the beach and some casualties were caused by mines. We pushed inland through a burning hayfield towards Les Roquettes, led by an ancient Boche who obligingly pointed out the path through the minefield. C Company reorganised at the farm and the Battalion Commander and CO of 90th Field appeared on the scene with another OP party from the regiment. We moved off towards Asnelles-sur-Mer through standing corn and hay, which gave good cover but caused a few separations more than once. We came across a platoon of Hampshires who were held up by machine-gun fire and got a fire order through to a ship for them. Perhaps it was as well that we had no OP truck. It would have attracted an awful lot of fire and we should have been pretty unpopular with the chaps on the ground.

'Germans could be seen running across open fields into their gunpits on Meuvaines ridge and bringing four 88-mm guns into action. Here was a target straight from heaven and, with as much calmness as we could muster, we called for fire from the ships; but they were all engaged on other targets and could only promise to engage as soon as possible. We cursed the Centaurs and made a mental note to ask for a LCG all to ourselves if ever we did another assault. We crawled into a field of clover to get a better view; some one shouted "You're in a minefield", and we withdrew somewhat daintily. Again and again, in an agony to get at those 88s, we called for fire, but the ships were still engaged on priority targets. Meanwhile the 88s were having a pretty successful open-sight shoot at our infantry as they doubled across a bit of open ground ahead. We got over intact, but two men of the Dorsets beside us were killed outright. About a mile further on the ships asked us to give them the result of their shoot on our target. We replied with restraint, "Unable to observe — now".

'Looking back at the beach we could see masses of men and vehicles pouring ashore, and the "Flails" were going into action to clear a lane through the minefield. They seemed to be touching off Teller mines most effectively.

'The wood on the high ground west of Buhot was a pre-selected rendezvous for commanders and FOOs. Here was to be laid on the fire plan for the attack on the defences west of Puits d'Hérode and the gun position 600 yards west of this elaborately prepared area. Both objectives were extremely clear in the air photos supplied before the landing. The wood, however, was strongly held and Spandaus sent us all hopping smartly into a ditch as soon as we took a look at the place. Two troops of 90th Field were now in action on the beaches and the target was duly registered and plastered good and proper as tanks and infantry moved forward across open country. The objective was taken, not without some trouble, and a good bag of prisoners was collected. Mortar bombs fell as soon as we occupied the wood, but did no damage.

'"A" Company, 1st Dorsets, was given the task of taking the defended locality to the west. The attack was timed to go in at 3 o'clock and we ranged a troop on to the target and gave the area 40 rounds as the attack went in. The guns were beautifully together and the infantry went right in close to the concentration and took the position without loss.

'We got left behind as a result of this shoot and had a series of minor adventures before we joined up again, not the least of which was the uncomfortable experience of being pinned to the ground for five minutes by an unseen Spandau enthusiast who had been lying doggo when the infantry passed him. But we eventually found C Company an hour later and arrived just in time to pass fire orders for B Troop Commander, who had lost both his signallers and his set to the 88s on Meuvaines ridge. He did some nice shooting and when the infantry went in the German guns had been abandoned. A small counterattack developed in our rear, but order was soon restored and more of the enemy put in the bag. We could have done with our OP truck by now. The signallers were pretty tired and had had a long carry and a lot of crawling. It was a great credit to them that our 68 set maintained communication with some station on the regimental net all day and part of the night.

'It was now evening and we set off across country towards the long ridge north of Ryes and met with no opposition at all. We joined up with the Devons, who were pulling out many prisoners from the dug-outs built into the steep railway embankment on the ridge, arranged DF tasks for the night with the battalion commanders and passed the information back to the guns by wireless, then established ourselves in a wonderful German command post of incredible depth and solidity. There we brewed the best cup of tea of all time and took a last look at the colossal armada anchored off the beaches, an unforgettable sight in the light of the setting sun.'

Capt Perring Thomas commanded B Troop, 41st Battery of 20th Anti-Tank Regiment, equipped with M10 SP 17/pdrs. They landed with 185th Infantry Brigade of 3rd Infantry Division at H-plus-four hours (11am), with the role of supporting the 2nd Battalion, King's Shropshire Light Infantry. The beach was congested with vehicles, its exit being partly blocked and under intermittent fire from the west. At about 1.15pm, however, Thomas's troop cleared the beach and set off up the brigade 'axis'.

Presently they came upon burning British tanks and 'walking-wounded' moving to the rear. Here they joined tanks of the Staffordshire Yeomanry, also looking for the infantry. While waiting for the Yeomanry to move forward they were fired upon ineffectively by a German mortar, which was spotted and silenced by one of the gun detachments. The Yeomanry now proposed to make a sweep to the east as a prelude to further advance and the anti-tank troop followed them. Thomas continues:

'The guns soon issued out on to the open plain in country very reminiscent of Salisbury Plain. The only cover existed in and around the villages, the open land being mainly tilled with growing corn. By this time it was late afternoon and shortly after arriving in this position gunfire was heard on the far side of the village of Bieville, some distance in rear of the Troop. Shortly afterwards two Mk IV Panzer tanks came out of cover about 2000 yards away in the direction of Perrier sur le Dan. Anti-tank training said the ideal fighting range was 800 yards and less. Fire should be held until the range closed. Accordingly the guns laid on the tanks and waited for the tanks to approach. Simultaneously with this incident other tanks must have been working their way forward in dead ground and two more tanks suddenly appeared in hull down position about half a mile away. They immediately opened fire on No 1 Gun and got two or three rounds away before the slow traverse of the SP M10s allowed the troop to reply. A slogging match now followed with the tanks rushing up to join in. The No 1 Gun was hit very early on by a round which struck at the join of the turret ring just above the driver's head. The sergeant was killed and the two gunners wounded, one dying ten days later in England. The Driver and wireless operator were unhurt and the SP was immediately backed off the position with the gun hanging helplessly over the front with both trunnions shattered.

'While this was going on the range of the original two tanks had not decreased and the order to engage was given before they disappeared entirely in the direction of the beaches. After a few ranging rounds at this unaccustomed distance hits began to be observed and very rapidly both Panzers were stopped and on fire.

'After this event the three remaining guns were re-deployed to cover the flank since it was clear that no further forward movement was likely that day. At last light the guns moved with the tanks into a defensive circle, ammunition was fetched up from the beaches, no one thought of sleep and, hourly, expected some interference from the enemy. A German Feldwebel gave himself up to the Yeomanry during the night, but nothing untoward happened. Before first light everything had moved and the Troop was deployed in the orchards west of Bieville in support of the KSLI. Stand-to passed off without incident.'

Subsequent accounts of this battle indicate it to have been a definite attempt by a German task force of 24 tanks to prepare the ground for a larger-scale attempt at a breakthrough, the latter being cancelled that evening.

In the succeeding days the invasion force poured ashore. In the British sector the Second (British) Army landed first, followed by the First (Canadian) Army. Until, in the first five days, something over a thousand guns of the Second Army had got ashore, a considerable load fell on the Naval guns offshore, their fire controlled by FOBs and often by ordinary ground

Early days in the Normandy beachhead

160
LAA defence of the artificial ('Mulberry') harbour. *IWM*
161
Auster IV of 652 Air OP Squadron being wheeled-out for take-off. *IWM*
162
155mm gun of 6 Heavy Battery. *J. F. Willcocks*
163
Abandoned German 88mm. *J. F. Willcocks*

and air OPs. Air OP reconnaissance parties were ashore on D+1 and, on D+2 (8 June), aircraft of two squadrons landed in the beach-head and started work immediately.

By 13 June, although the town of Caen had not, as hoped, been captured in the first rush, a British-American bridgehead existed some 50 miles long and 8-12 miles deep.

And, early on 13 June, the first of the V1 'flying bombs' was launched against south-east England and descended on the north Kent coast. By the 16th the AOC Fighter Command, with overall responsibility for the air defence of the Country, had ordered the planned deployment to take place. Within 24 hours almost 400 AA guns had been deployed and by the end of the month the 'gun-zone' contained almost 1,600 guns, three quarters of which were LAA.

By the middle of July some 3,000 flying-bombs (or V1s or doodle-bugs) had entered the main defended sector. Fighters had destroyed 900, guns 250, balloons 55. Of the remaining 1,800, 1,270 had reached London. AA gunners had always yearned for targets which flew at constant course, speed and height; now they had got them in lavish numbers but results were disappointing.

The American radars, predictors and VT fuzes, however, were now appearing in quantity. The fuzes could not be used over land since they incorporated no effective self-destructive arrangements; the radars and predictors, however, offered substantial improvement. Maj-Gen B. P. Hughes, writing in the *Royal Artillery Journal* of September 1971, mentions a third notable factor, arising out of interference by fighter aircraft and guns with each other's activities:

'In the first weeks of the battle it had proved extremely difficult to prevent these two elements from impeding each other in the limited areas in which the target had to be engaged. The Air Officer Commanding-in-Chief, Air Marshal Sir Roderick Hill, was in fact at this point considering the ways in which interference between fighters and guns could be eliminated when his Deputy Senior Air Staff Officer, Air Commodore Geoffrey Ambler, reappreciating the whole problem from the joint service angle, suggested that the defences as a whole would be more effective if the whole of the gun belt was moved to the coast. The fighters could then operate both in front of and behind them. The guns would have a clear field of fire and furthermore it would be possible to use the VT fuze over the sea.

'General Pile and his staff had in fact already thought of such a scheme but had felt that it would be too revolutionary to propose. When therefore the GOC in C was called to a conference with the AOC in C and heard

164
Gen Sir Frederick Pile, C-in-C
AA Command throughout the
war, his Maj-Gen of the
General Staff, Whittaker, and
the Prime Minister. *IWM*

165
ACM Sir Roderick Hill, C-in-C
Fighter Command, responsible
for the conduct of the battle
against the V1s. *IWM*

166
The V1. *IWM*

the new plan suggested he welcomed it
unreservedly.'

The revised lay-out was adopted on 15
and 16 July. Lifted from holdfasts all
over Britain, 400 Mark IIC guns were
by dawn on the 17th on 'Pile Plat-
forms' in the coastal belt; slightly less
than 600 LAA guns were in action
there 48 hours later. Gen Hughes adds:
'It will readily be appreciated that the
move itself was a most remarkable
feat, involving not only the transport of
a mass of heavy equipment not
designed primarily for mobility but
also the many complexities of an
entirely new signals layout, together
with the necessary administrative
rearrangements for a force of 23,000
men and women with 60,000 tons of
ammunition and stores. But the
immediate result of this tour de force
was a startling improvement in the
performance of the defences.'

By the third week in August over 40%
of the V1s were being destroyed and of
these the guns were destroying over
half. Searchlights too were playing a
significant part in the RAF's destruction of night-flying V1s.

For an eye-witness impression of the
view from the guns, we can do worse
than quote, from Henry Longhurst's *I
Wouldn't Have Missed It*, a passage in
which he describes a night's visit to an
HAA site on the Kent coast and the air
of expectancy that came with the
dawn:
'Any minute now! At last, far, far away
in the dawn, there appears a tiny pale
light, for all the world like the first
morning star. It is moving very slightly
across the sky, even as another star,
not bearing man's devices of death,
may have moved over Bethlehem
2,000 years before. But such thoughts
follow afterwards. For the moment all
we know is "This is it!" and in a
minute or so, in that purposeful sort of
way that doodles have, the first target
of the day comes hurrying along.

'A second later a fantastic cannonade shatters the silence. From
every open space within miles men are
shooting at this thing. Deafening
cracks, accompanied by sheets of
flame, rock our wooden platform.
Black puffs smudge the sky all round
the doodle, some desperately near,
some not so good, one or two, where a
man has mis-set his fuze, far wide of
the mark. It seems incredible that anything can live in this, but it does. On it
flies, and now the Bofors are in range.
For men who have not had a target for
a year and then only the quick ten-
second flash of a Focke-Wulf, this is
their dream come true. Their tracers
climb into the sky in hundreds and I
find myself in a burst of fellow-feeling

167
The random misery of the
flying bombs. Human
catastrophe in North London.
IWM

168
Bombardier F. Cary, who had
one of the earliest successes in
the flying bomb battle when he
brought down a V1 with
machine gun fire. *IWM*

thinking of the respective No 4s with their foot clamped down on the foot pedal, ramming the shells into the autoloader. It seems that even now the doodle will get away with it, but suddenly someone gets it. Throwing its head back for all the world like a pheasant, it glides to earth and goes off with a colossal orange flash somewhere back on the marshes.

'Never mind that now. Look out, here comes another! The cannonade goes on. Almost the first salvo hits it, and a mile out to sea it disintegrates in mid-air, inaudible against the noise of the guns. Another is on its tail. This makes a more dramatic exit. Someone knocks out its gyro control and sets it on fire. Fizzing like a comet and leaving a long trail of black smoke, it careers drunkenly upwards, loses impetus and spirals into the sea.'

Meanwhile the Normandy bridgehead slowly expanded. The Americans captured Cherbourg on 26 June, though its harbour facilities were not available for some time. Between the 25th and 29th the British thrust west of Caen and over the River Odon, a feature of this advance being the heavy artillery concentrations. As Parham put it (he was now BRA — British Second Army), 'the enemy within gun range lived under a constant threat of encountering a sudden squall of several hundred shell, all timed to arrive at the target end within a few seconds of each other'. The Air OPs played a prominent part in promoting such squalls, one of the more notable being a shoot by Maj Andrew Lyell, OC No 658 Squadron, against a collection of enemy tanks in harbour. The artillery of three corps, 500-600 field, medium and heavy guns, took part in this shoot.

On 8 July an offensive was launched to capture Caen. This was preceded, on the evening before, by large-scale Bomber Command raids on targets on

The Redeployment

169
Laying a Pile platform,
Hastings. *IWM*
170
3.7in Mark IIC gun being
towed on to the platform.
IWM
171
450 Mixed HAA Battery in
action, Romney Marsh, Kent.
*Brig B. Chichester-Cooke and
Sport & General Press Agency*

Anti-tank action in the Normandy beachhead

172
Panther tank, burning. *IWM*
173
17pdr detachment of 146 Anti-
tank Battery — satisfied.
IWM

174
Bofors detachment of 102 LAA
Regiment making use of
former enemy emplacement.
IWM

the northern edge of the town, and these were preceded by a massive and successful artillery fire programme against located enemy AA guns. The Germans withdrew from Caen on the 9th, but the devastation from the bombing made consolidation slow.

From 18 to 20 July, in Operation 'Goodwood', the British Second Army attacked east and south-east of Caen. 317th Battery of 165th HAA Regiment, with mobile 3.7in guns, took part in the formidable artillery neutralisation-programme, particularly against the enemy's flak (AA) sites during the opening bomber offensive. Capt S. L. E. Andrews, commander of F Troop of this battery, had served therein for almost three years, in Britain, during which it had fired in anger only four times; from now on, while AA engagements were hardly more frequent than before, they (like many other HAA units) were regularly in action as long-range field artillery. Andrews has well described the scene at his troop position during the overture to 'Goodwood'.

'Our guns were by now going flat out on to the pre-selected targets — dust and smoke filled the sky and there was an acrid smell of cordite overall in the calm morning air; the gunners worked like men possessed, stripped to the waist, their forearms protected by the massive leather loading gloves which prevented injury when ramming home the 56-lb brass cartridges and shells; layers kept the guns trained on the correct bearing and elevation while the sergeants in charge were constantly acknowledging and relaying orders from the command post, shouting themselves hoarse above the din of battle.

'As each gunner rammed home his round he stepped smartly to his right,

175
Warlike scene in the billeting area — Bombardier Thomas (left) and Sgt Coyne fielding, the batswoman's name is not recorded. *IWM*

176
Winching a 5.5 from its pit — 68 Medium Regiment. *IWM*

hand on the firing lever, awaiting his No 1's order to fire; after each discharge the gun would recoil for its full thirty inches, run back into the cradle, the breech would automatically be thrown open and out would fly the ejected cartridge case to be neatly fielded by the firer and tossed over the gunpit wall in one quick action where a pile of cases some four feet in height began to accumulate. At some time later in the morning some RAF radar-operators from a nearby locating site volunteered their services as loaders and this offer was gratefully accepted. The sun became obscured by the dense clouds of dust and smoke that rose towards heaven, the gunners were unrecognisable under their thick layer of dust and cordite-carbon, the guns' barrels became red-hot and the oil in the buffer section of the recoil system boiled.'

The neutralisation of the enemy's flak was successful, but the bombing programme notably failed to subdue the enemy's field and anti-tank artillery and the offensive made only limited gains at some cost.

During the fighting in the bridgehead during the past six weeks the most anxious artillery factor was the high casualty-rate in the anti-tank regiments. The German Panther was now reinforcing the Tiger tank and replacing earlier models; the new British anti-tank guns (SP or towed) were ready for this, but not perhaps for the inherent tactical dangers for slow-moving guns from well-concealed enemy guns and tanks. Besides British guns, however, many German tanks were destroyed and relatively few encountered in subsequent battles.

The American 'break-out' started

177
Mortar victims in the
beachhead — 17pdr and
tractor. *IWM*

178
Sexton 25pdr gun (probably of
76 Field Regiment) in action
east of Caen. *IWM*

spectacularly on 25 July, reaching
Avranches, 80 miles south of Cherbourg, on the 30th. Detaching a corps
to clear Brittany, the Americans
wheeled south-east. Von Kluge, now
the German commander, launched his
panzer divisions upon the left flank of
the American advance, north of
Avranches. Montgomery quickly
sensed the opportunity thus created to
surround a major part of the German
army in Normandy; while the
Canadian First Army (now complete in
the bridgehead) attacked southwards
towards Falaise, Bradley was instructed to swing part of his army
northwards.

As the German armour strove to dis-
engage itself and escape east through
the narrowing 'Falaise Gap' a deluge of
fire descended upon them from the
Allied cannon and rocket-firing aircraft
and from artillery. The best testimony
must be that of a German participant,
such as Gen Heinrich von Lüttwitz,
commander of 2nd Panzer Division, as
quoted in Milton Shulman's *Defeat in
the West*. Von Lüttwitz refers to his
increasing casualties from air and
artillery attacks on 19 August, the

179
The Falaise Gap. *IWM*

increasing heaps of shattered horses and vehicles, and the order received by him that evening to break-out near St Lambert. He dispatched his remaining fifteen tanks as vanguard but soon discovered the impossibility of night-driving among so many destroyed vehicles. His columns set off again at 4am and Lüttwitz was surprised to encounter little artillery fire. He continues:

'In this lull we began to move in the early-morning mist of August 20th. As a narrow lane near St Lambert was known still to provide an escape route across the Dives river, columns of all the encircled units were streaming towards it, some of them driving in rows of eight vehicles abreast. Suddenly at seven o'clock in the morning the artillery fire, which had been so silent, now broke out into a storm such as I had never before experienced. Alongside the Dives the numerous trains of vehicles ran into direct enemy fire of every description, turned back, and in some cases drove round in a circle until they were shot-up and blocked the roads. Towering pillars of smoke rose incessantly from petrol tanks as they were hit, ammunition exploded, riderless horses stampeded, some of them badly wounded. Organised direction was no longer possible, and only a few of my tanks and infantry got through to St Lambert.'

On 15 August the United States Seventh Army had landed in the south of France, whence the Germans withdrew skilfully enough to prevent them from contributing much to Allied operations further north. There the Seine was the next target. The United States Third Army crossed it north and south of Paris, on 20 and 23 August; early on the 25th Free French and American forces, amid scenes of delirious excitement, reached the centre of the French capital.

Other Seine bridgeheads were quickly established and in the north, with Gen Horrocks's XXX Corps in the lead, there began an exhilarating pursuit which took the British two hundred miles to Brussels, the heart of Belgium, by the afternoon of 3 September and to Antwerp on the following day. The Army's sudden arrival in these cities created a strange mixture of war and celebration which resulted in many unusual situations.

Antwerp, for some days after 'liberation', was shelled by German artillery north of the River Scheldt. As a prelude to counter-action a flash-spotting troop was deployed in the city to locate the enemy batteries. The writer, under the pseudonym 'Alice', of an article in *Gunner* magazine of January 1945 had military reasons to watch the counter-bombardment programme and obtained permission to observe from one of the flash-spotting OPs which, he was informed, was on the top floor of an Antwerp hotel. He drove there and found the hotel to be 'an establishment of the Ritz-Carlton type and still in full running order'.

'Alice' stood in the hall in some embarrassment; it hardly seemed the way to a flash-spotting OP in action against the enemy. But help was at hand.

'A field-marshal of the Ruritanian Army approached me and asked if he could help me. It dawned on me that he was the hall porter — though at this stage in the war it would hardly have been surprising if he had been a field-marshal in the Ruritanian Army. It was all quite mad, so I decided to lose my wits too, and to ask him quite seriously if he could direct me to the OP.

'Evidently lunacy was common sense here. ''If you will take the lift, sir, the pageboy will show you the way.'' I entered the gilt and mirrored lift and the boy in charge pressed the topmost button.

'We stopped and the buttons threw open the gates with a flourish. I stepped out into a large room which must have been a dining-room until a few days ago. It was elaborately decorated, tables and chairs were stacked at one side, there was a dais where a band must have played and a bar in one corner still held glasses and ashtrays but, alas, no bottles.

'There were large French windows on two sides of the room. Sitting in armchairs — from the stock at the other side of the room — looking out of the windows, with their instruments on the small balconies outside, was the FS party. Antwerp was spread out below them and in the middle distance stretched the country across the river where the enemy batteries were.'

As the Allied armies advanced across France and Belgium, the enemy moved their V1 launching sites into Holland, and also launched from aircraft over

180
Gun Operations Room (GOR) at HQ 57 AA Brigade, near Saxmundham, Suffolk, specifically tailored to the V1 battle in its final phase. The brigade commander, standing centre right, was Brig Chichester-Cooke. *IWM*

181
REME Workshop in support of AA Command. Brig Chichester-Cooke paid particular tribute in the *RA Commemoration Book* to REME's tirelessness in the help they gave with the installation and maintenance of the new equipment. *IWM*

the North Sea. The AA defences had to be reorientated by successive redeployments and extended up the east coast as far as Great Yarmouth. At the same time the V2 rocket began to appear (or rather to arrive without appearing); there was no defence against this weapon except to discover and bomb its launching sites.

The V1 destruction-rate continued to rise and by 11 September had reached a figure of 83%. Brig B. Chichester-Cooke, who commanded 57th AA Brigade, writes in the *RA Commemoration Book* of a subtle change in the 'next morning' messages from Group to Brigade HQ. 'From being congratulatory on the number of doodles destroyed, they developed into requests for the reason why a *certain flying bomb* had penetrated the defences. Perhaps this was the highest form of praise.'

After the capture of Brussels the British 21st Army Group had two objects in view — first, the clearance of the territory north of the Scheldt estuary and the opening thereby of the port of Antwerp and, secondly, with the American forces, to maintain the momentum of the advance on Germany. The Germans had created strong fortifications — the Siegfried Line — along their frontiers with Luxembourg and Belgium but further north, along the Dutch frontier, the defences were less strong. Montgomery favoured an ambitious thrust north of the Siegfried Line, using British and American airborne forces simultaneously to seize the bridges over the Maas, Waal and Neder Rijn in the path of the advancing British Second Army. To the British 1st Airborne Division fell the lot of capturing the northernmost of these objectives — the bridge over the Neder Rijn at Arnhem.

This operation, including subsequent supply, employed thousands of aircraft sorties, and it was not possible for 1st Division to be flown-in in a single day's lift — possibly the decisive weakness in the plan. The division's artillery consisted of no more than 1st Airlanding Light Regiment (three batteries of 75mm howitzers) and 1st and 2nd Airlanding Anti-Tank batteries (one with 17pdrs and the other with 6pdrs). There were parachute-dropped OP parties to direct the fire of the 75mms and also of the Second Army artillery as it advanced from the south and came within range of Arnhem. Lt-Col W. F. K. Thompson (years later to become familiar to many as military correspondent of the *Daily Telegraph*) was CO of the Light Regiment. The operation began on 17 September.

Lt-Col R. G. Loder-Symonds was CRA of the Division and Maj Philip Tower, his brigade-major, wrote for the *RA Commemoration Book*:

'The arrival was on time, the parachute OPs both of the Light Regiment and of the Forward Observer Unit jumping with the battalions, and the glider-borne 75mms and anti-tank guns coming in on their own landing zone. The only casualties appeared to be a few of the huge Hamilcar gliders, which tipped up on landing on a potato field that proved rougher than expected. Even from some of these, on their backs, their 17-pdrs and tractors were successfully removed.

'That afternoon was quiet; the 1st and 3rd Light Batteries were in action together, and supported the advance of 1 Parachute Brigade towards the Arnhem bridge, six miles away. Some anti-tank guns of 1st Anti-tank Battery accompanied the brigade, others stayed with 1 Airlanding Brigade, who were guarding the drop zones until 4 Parachute Brigade could arrive on the 18th.

'That night saw the arrival of part of 1 Parachute Brigade at the bridge, and with it a troop of 6-pdrs of 1st Anti-tank Battery (Major W. F. Arnold). Soon, after a brisk fight, the bridge fell into our hands and the 6-pdrs were in action on its northern end. So far, so good; but the whole brigade was not there and by the middle of the next day the enemy had definitely blocked its advance. Meantime 3rd Light Battery had moved to Oosterbeek, three miles from the bridge and a few hundred yards from the north bank of the Neder Rijn. From this position the brigade could be supported, and here the whole regiment was to fight its battle.

'During the afternoon 4 Parachute Brigade arrived, with its 2nd Anti-tank Battery; and despite having to fight scattered enemy on its drop zone, was able to move off towards Arnhem that evening. With it came 2nd Light Battery, thus completing the Light Regiment, which by then had 23 guns in action.

'That night and the following day were to be the period of tragedy: the initiative was lost, and from then on

Arnhem, September 1944

182
1 Airlanding Light Regiment in action (75mm gun) near Oosterbeek. *IWM*

183
Lt-Col W. F. K. Thompson, CO of 1 Airlanding Light Regiment.
Brig W. F. K. Thompson

the Division first defended and was finally to be fighting for its life. Two attacks went in, one along the river at night to reach the beleaguered garrison at the bridge, one on the 19th to the north by 4th Parachute Brigade to capture the rest of the town.

'Both were supported by all guns of the Light Regiment. Both ran into completely unexpected German positions and tanks, and both ended in failure. 2nd Anti-tank Battery (Major Haynes) shared the discomfiture of 4 Parachute Brigade; many OP parties, Light Regiment and FOU were lost, and by the evening the Division perforce began to form its defence perimeter, leaving the bridge garrison to fight it out alone.

'To conform, the 1st and 2nd Light Batteries (Major A. F. Norman-Walker and Major J. E. F. Linton respectively) were moved to Oosterbeek into the area of 3rd Light Battery (Major D. S. Munford), which was already fast losing its character of a peaceful gun position. The complete failure of the southern attack on Arnhem resulted in numerous parties of infantry and anti-tank gunners withdrawing in comparative confusion into the area, where they were collected, rallied and re-deployed in most exemplary fashion by Lieutenant-Colonel Thompson. This mixed force, reinforced by glider pilots, now defended a line which in places was coincident with the gun positions, and as a whole was to prove one of the key points of the whole divisional perimeter.

'The next day, Wednesday September 20th, was the first of the defensive phase. The parachutists holding the bridge, three miles away, were now completely cut off from the rest of the Division in its perimeter at Oosterbeek, and though the troop of 1st Anti-tank Battery with them did great execution amongst enemy vehicles attempting to cross, they were unable to prevent four German Tiger tanks forcing their way through the now greatly depleted defenders of the bridge.

'On Thursday the 21st, with few unwounded, without ammunition and food, they tried to fight their way out, but were all killed or captured. The defence of the bridge was over.'

From then onwards the Oosterbeek position was defended against increasing enemy attacks by infantry and tanks, mortars and machine-guns. On the 21st, however, radio contact was made with 64th Medium Regiment of XXX Corps, deployed at Nijmegen. From then onwards its heavier fire support was available, to be joined by other Second Army artillery as it advanced within range. The anti-tank guns were employed around the perimeter but their numbers steadily diminished and ammunition fell short.

Lt-Col Thompson, who had been a tower of strength to his regiment and to the division, was wounded on 21st and evacuated to a 'Dressing station' which the enemy later overran. On the 22nd the enemy penetrated all three battery areas and were ejected only after fierce fighting; the perimeter shrank as two batteries withdrew closer to the river.

For the end of this battle we turn again to Maj Tower:
'It could not go on for ever; on the ninth day since the Division had landed with such high hopes, Field-Marshal Montgomery himself ordered the withdrawal of the survivors.

'A tremendous fire plan was arranged with XXX Corps over the slender radio link from HQRA, the Division's main touch with the outside world. As this began, at 10 p.m on the night of the 25th, the remaining defenders began to steal down to the river where Canadian boats awaited them. All through that night, as the Germans awaited the assault from the south across the river, which they thought was heralded by the firing, boatload after boatload slipped across to rest and safety.

'Last of the Division to go was the Light Regiment. Sadly, breech-blocks and sights, even those of the guns overrun by the enemy, were removed and dropped in the river. As day dawned and the enemy, realising at last his mistake, began to machine-gun the river-banks. Major de Gex, now in command of the regiment, took the last boatload across. Soon hit, it sank, and he joined the RSM and Major Linton in the river, which they, like many others, were compelled to swim.'

The Canadian First Army, meanwhile, had reduced the by-passed fortresses of Boulogne and Calais and cleared the Scheldt estuary. The British artillery's part in the Boulogne operation may be mentioned as an historical oddity, consisting as it did of a five-day neutralisation of the German coast and railway guns at Cap Gris Nez, to the east of the town. The British artillery employed were the 15in and 14in coast guns at

Dover and observation of fire was by Air OP, 23 miles away across the Channel. Parham and Belfield, describing operations of 18 September in their Air OP history, remark: 'That day ended with the pilot engaging, with his great weapons in England, an enemy flak battery which had been bothering him — a somewhat awe-inspiring form of personal reprisal!,

There remained Dunkirk; Gen Hughes, who by then commanded 51st AA Defence Group, defending 21 Army Group's base and lines of communication, recalls as follows:
'While no one bothered very much about the German garrison of Dunkirk which had been bypassed and contained there, it was clear that it was being supplied by air at night. 85 Group of the Royal Air Force, which was responsible for the night air defence of all the rearward areas, was naturally interested, and, assuming that the supply-dropping aircraft were approaching at low altitude over the sea, arranged patrols of night fighters and radar observation. No trace of any German aircraft could be found.

'One night I was standing with the Commanding Officer of one of the night fighter squadrons of 85 Group on his airfield well inland when we heard an aircraft approaching at low altitude. Looking up we saw, some 50 feet above us, the unmistakable plan view of a German He111 flying north east. The bell rang simultaneously, and we realised that this was one of the Dunkirk supply droppers following a route that had not been suspected owing to the difficulty then of flying overland at a very low altitude at night. (It was established later this was one of a specialised German Squadron composed of very experienced night fighter pilots using radio altimeters.)

'85 Group had been provided with six newly formed LAA/SL batteries for the defence of its airfields. A quick word with the AOC, who gave his agreement to the prising-out of four of those batteries from their normal tasks, and they were in action round the Dunkirk perimeter by the following night.

'Supply dropping was attempted on five more successive nights by 12 aircraft operating in groups of 2 to 4 at a time. Of these, four were illuminated by searchlights and destroyed on the

Brig B. P. Hughes, commanding 51 AA Defence Group, at an Armistice Day ceremony at Hesdin, northern France, where his HQ was situated. Beside him, M. le Maire. *Maj-Gen B. P. Hughes*

spot by LAA guns, one was probably destroyed, and two damaged. Two more flew into the ground when dazzled by searchlights.'

The British Second Army now closed up to the line of the River Maas and repulsed a German counter-thrust at the end of October, when 25th Field Regiment supported the United States 7th Armored Division in a two-day battle in which artillery firepower was the key.

By their prevention of the breakthrough to Arnhem, however, the Germans had stabilised their western front and on 16 December were even able to take the offensive against the Americans in the Ardennes with a powerful thrust aimed north-west at Brussels and Antwerp. This carried them 50 miles to a glimpse of the River Meuse at Dinant, but stout American defence and counter-offensive held and then repulsed them and by the end of 1944 the threat was over.

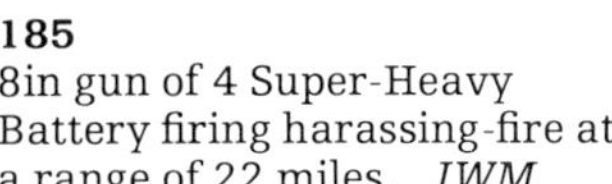

185
8in gun of 4 Super-Heavy Battery firing harassing-fire at a range of 22 miles. *IWM*

186
5.5s of 233 Battery, 68 Medium Regiment, supporting Polish troops across the River Maas, January 1945. *IWM*

10 The End

Germany's position was now hopeless; Russians, Americans and British closed in inexorably. Hitler, however, intended to fight on, an indication of this being the continuance of missile attacks on London and, since October 1944, on Antwerp and Brussels also. While the United States army took over the air defence of Antwerp, that of Brussels remained the responsibility of 21st Army Group and employed seven HAA regiments (including three Mixed regiments), one LAA and part of one SL regiment. Until the end of February 1945, when attacks on Brussels ceased, AA results were excellent — except of course against the V2s, by which unfortunately many Dutch and Belgians were killed.

The V1 attacks on London continued for a further month during which, of 257 missiles launched, only 125 reached the defences, 87 being destroyed by guns and four by fighters and only 13 reaching the capital.

In the first week of March, after the Canadian First Army, with XXX British Corps under command, had overcome obstinate resistance in the Lower Rhineland, the Allied armies reached the Rhine. On the evening of 23 March 3,300 guns fired a two-hour pre-

187
3.7in Battery of 481 (Mixed) HAA Regiment occupying a position in the AA defence of Brussels, early 1945. *IWM*

liminary bombardment of the Rhine's eastern bank on the 25 miles of the 21st Army Group front. Lt-Col G. B. Thatcher, CO of 20th Anti-Tank Regiment, describes the scene in an account written for the *RA Commemoration Book*:

'It is about eleven o'clock on the morning of Friday, March 23rd, 1945. To-night the Rhine is going to be crossed — but not by me. My Regiment is supporting from this bank. We are taking part in a "Pepperpot".

'Things are very quiet at the moment though we are only a couple of miles from the river. I have a pleasant little house as regimental command post. From my bedroom window I shall be able to see most of my guns. The cellar is reinforced concrete, and in it live all the telephones, wireless sets, etc. Two of my batteries are coming into action in this area presently, but they are not allowed to start digging before noon. A Canadian field regiment has decided to come here too, though it is far out of its proper area. I haven't the heart to remonstrate, because they've done all their survey now. Anyway, it's too fine to quarrel. There will be a tremendous conglomeration of guns round here tonight, however.

'There is still a smoke screen all down the Rhine, so the Huns can't see what we are doing. And I haven't seen an enemy plane over for several days. It is said they've got one of our Air OPs and are using it. I wonder — or is it just the MGRA again?

'Here come the digging and camouflaging parties; we've seven hours before we are due to fire. There are six 17-pdrs to be dug in and 12 SP Valentines to be concealed in this area. It is a lovely afternoon. I think I'll sleep in the sun. There is nothing for me to do; everything has been worked out for the fire plan. The survey is complete, communications seem to be OK, and luckily there is no office bumph.

'I've just noticed there's a 17-pdr pointing straight at my bedroom window. He'll clear the house, however, because he is firing reduced charge — that is to say, if he remembers to level his bubble.

'I wonder how my chaps are going to do; being an anti-tank regiment we haven't done much of this indirect stuff, and this is the first real full-blooded predicted party we've taken on. They'll be all right, but I wish it was going to be in daylight. I hope the wind doesn't change, because if it

does, it'll blow all our own smoke screen back over us, and apart from obscuring everything it makes us cough and feel very sick. At least, it did last night.

'Six well-directed shells have just hit someone else's ammunition dump. We hear the guns fire and take a bearing, which is sent to HQRA. Things are not so quiet now. It is five o'clock and our counter-battery has started. The Canadian 25-pdrs open up, the right-hand gun of their right-hand troop is only five yards from my left-hand SP. This area is lousy with guns; you can't turn round for them.

'Two hours to go before we fire. The order is no brewing up in the open, so my chaps have gone back to a farm for tea. My two outlying batteries report they are quite happy — I am through to them by line and wireless; long may it continue so, though the "air" is getting pretty chaotic. We are firing from H-120 to H-5, that is from 7.0 pm to 8.55 pm — 2,700 rounds of 17-pdr. But that's a mere fleabite compared to the rest of the "Pepperpot". The Bofors are going to fire over 50,000 rounds in the same period. Then there are the 4.2-inch mortars and two squadrons of tanks, to say nothing of the machine guns.

'Time to walk round the nearby batteries; they seem all right and full of confidence, though they are undertaking something they've never done before. Everyone in very good heart; and so back to the cellar and centre of communications. All lines are still through, and there appears to be very little coming back in the way of enemy shelling. The time creeps on. I must see the opening of this party from upstairs. I reckon that during the first few seconds there ought to be something like 500 rounds in the air, all together and all tracer. Those are "Pepperpot" rounds, all landing in a fairly restricted area just over the Rhine. Goodness knows how many divisional artillery mediums and heavies will be firing as well.

'And so up to the balcony to watch. Fifteen seconds to go . . . ten . . . five . . . there goes one of my SP Troops; they're a few seconds early — not that you'd notice it, because almost immediately the sky seems to be crammed full of tracer. Bofors pumping away from in front, from the sides and over our heads from behind. With their flat trajectory they seem to be skimming the housetops. 17-pdrs have a more sober air as, with reduced charge and comparatively high trajectory, they sail gracefully away into the night sky, the tracer burning out long before the round falls. I am quite sure of one thing; our war correspondents will run out of adjectives long before we run out of ammunition. It is terrific; by far the best thing I've ever seen. More impressive than D-day — and makes the Crystal Palace seem like table fireworks. I could watch this for hours, but I musn't idle about up here, so down to the cellar to ''see'' what is really happening. All batteries shot on serial one, now firing serial two. Everything is going like clockwork, except that the line to HQRA has gone, though we are still through by wireless.

'I wish I could go out and around the guns, but if I leave this place I know something will happen to require my presence here. In the meantime there's no harm in popping up on the balcony again. These fireworks are worth watching. The inferno has increased, if anything. Field and medium guns are still firing, but even their noise is drowned by the ''Pepperpot'' guns. It is quite impossible to sort out what's coming from where, but it is all landing in the right direction. Those four rounds which swan away all on their own, right high up in the sky, separate from the common herd — yes, that must be E Troop firing on Rees. That's about the line and it is extreme range.

'Regiment shot on serial five; we rest for ten minutes now. Soon George comes in. He has been round the guns. He says the gunners are in tremendous heart and brewing tea during the rest. Lights don't matter at this stage!

'I notice the signallers down here keep relieving each other — theoretically to drink tea and smoke, I suppose, but in fact to have a look at the fireworks.

'Time is drawing near now; serial 11 finishes the party as far as we are concerned and at 8.55 to the tick come reports from batteries, ''Serial 11 shot. Guns empty''. The tumult dies as abruptly as it started, leaving the 25-pdrs and mediums to continue their more orthodox noise.

'And so to supper off a clean white table cloth and the voice of the BBC hinting at momentous events on the lower Rhine. They're telling us!'

By dawn on the 24th Allied troops were everywhere established on the east bank of the river, bridges were being constructed and anti-tank guns were employed in the unusual role of destroying floating mines launched by the enemy against the bridges. At 10am British and United States airborne formations landed beyond the bridgehead, after an artillery counter-flak programme which unfortunately was less than 100% successful. By evening, however, all the airborne objectives had been won and held. British and American bridgeheads were swiftly enlarged and consolidated, bridges were completed, troops, guns, ammunition — all poured across; and by 28 March the Allied armies were advancing across Germany against only spasmodic resistance. While the Canadians cleared north-east Holland, the British Second Army advanced to the River Elbe and crossed it on 29 April. The Russians were by now fighting in the Berlin suburbs and the drama of Hitler's bunker was approaching its final act.

On 4 May, on Luneberg Heath, General-Admiral von Friedeburg signed an armistice agreement and surrendered to Field-Marshal Montgomery all the armed forces in North-West Germany.

On 9 April 1945, with 21st Army Group already east of the Rhine, the British-American 15th Army Group once more took the offensive in Italy. The Eighth Army, now under Gen Sir Richard McCreery, attacked across the River Senio, east of Bologna, and on the 14th the Fifth Army attacked the German positions in the north-east Appenines. Bologna was occupied and on the 23rd the last of the river lines, that of the River Po, was attacked by both armies together.

German soldiers were still prepared to offer determined resistance but all cohesion had gone. 178th (Lowland) Medium Regiment, of 7th AGRA, was supporting 10th United States Mountain Division of Fifth Army; early on 23 April, after two days and nights of rapid advance, the Regiment's batteries were in action just south of the Po. A quick decision was made to cross the river and at noon the boats of the leading infantry set-off. The CO of 178th Regiment, Lt-Col H. S. Freeth, wrote an account of this day for the *RA Commemoration Book*, from which the following extract is taken:
'The chief opposition came from the devastating 88-mm low air-burst fire

190
317 Battery of 165 HAA Regiment take the first heavy guns across the River Elbe. *IWM*

191
Italy, 29 April 1945, The Gunner General Sir William Morgan, Chief-of-Staff Allied Force HQ, signs the Instrument of Surrender of the German forces. *IWM*

over the forming-up area, and later over the crossing itself — delivered, as we afterwards learned, by no less than 20 enemy guns. Men were falling fast, but in that flat country there was no hope of locating the guns, which were firing flashless ammunition so that even the Air OPs could not see them. In desperation the CO drove his jeep through the enemy fire to the river-bank. There he met three Austrian prisoners and an Italian youth, who had just been brought back by boats returning from the first flight. The Austrians only knew the infantry pos-itions, but the Italian youth had actually helped to dig the gunpits of the German guns. He was able to give their position on a 1/50,000 map, and they were promptly engaged with airburst, not only by 178th Medium plus Q Battery, but by 2nd Medium Regiment, which had by then closed up as well — a ''Yoke'' target from 40 medium guns! This fire soon silenced the enemy guns and enabled the infantry to secure a firm bridge-head. It was later found that the enemy had blown up all 20 88-mm guns in their pits.'

The advance continued to Lake Garda,

70 miles east of Milan, where the demolition of tunnels had blocked the main road. The infantry took to the water and outflanked the enemy rearguards; the Gunners requisitioned sailing barges to move their 5.5in guns up the lake, in continued support of the infantry until, on 2nd May, the German armies in Italy surrendered.

Now only Burma remained.

Burma

In Burma, as 1944 drew to its close, British-Indian forces were moving forward, both across the Chindwin and down the Arakan coast. 25th Indian Division of XV Corps, in the van of the latter offensive, made fast progress and on Boxing Day had reached the tip of the Mayu peninsula, to gaze across a narrow strip of water at the two-year old objective of Akyab Island. The island had been well fortified; an amphibious operation and much bloody fighting was expected before its capture and steps had been taken to assemble a formidable concentration of fire power. In addition to a regiment of 25pdrs, a battery of 5.5s, a section of 7.2s and two HAA batteries, almost certain to be available against surface targets, the Royal Navy was providing the gunfire of ten warships and the RAF the bombs or cannon of 22 squadrons. A coordinated fireplan had been made, with 25th Divisional HQ the 'controllers'; D-day was to be 3 January 1945.

The individuals who brought these plans to naught were Brig John Daniell, CRA 25th Division, Capt Jimmy Jarrett, RA, commander of C Flight of 656 Air OP Squadron and Gnr 'Derk' Carter, his batman.

On New Year's Day there were indications of unusual events on the island and Daniell briefed Jarrett to reconnoitre the planned target areas to see if they were occupied by civilians. Jarrett reconnoitred early next morning. Indeed the target areas were occupied by the Akyabis in some numbers, flags were on the rooftops and others were being waved. The airfield appeared mined but, north-east of the town, a large assembly had been marshalled clear of some sort of aircraft landing area. Jimmy Jarrett gave it a good look and landed, was informed that the Japanese had left, gave assurance in return that the British were coming soon, as friends, took-off and returned to John Daniell.

To Daniell, Jarrett and others on the spot, there was no doubt that the bombardment programme had to be cancelled. This was an inter-service matter, however, and needed high-level agreement. The staffs at those high levels, unaffected by local forebodings of the scenes on Akyab island after the bombardment and evidently unconcerned about waste of ammunition, were suspicious of Jap trickery and reluctant, anyway, to forego useful training for future tri-Service operations. Incredulous local commanders began to fear that the operation might go ahead as planned. 'I spent my time', records John Daniell, 'in quelling an almost mutiny among my OCs and Air OP officers who refused to take part in any fireplan aimed at Jimmy's friends on the island'.

As negotiations continued, Jimmy Jarrett was asked to fly over again and see if he could bring back a local 'spokesman'. He took with him Gnr Carter and, this time, having landed, he switched off the engine. Jarrett's account, in the *RA Commemoration Book*, continues:

'...the crowd surged round — swamped the aircraft, shouting "Three Cheers" for the British Empire, King George VI, Churchill — and me! All shaking hands, talking and shouting at once and waving home-made paper flags of the Union Jack, Stars and Stripes and Tricolour. To my horror, I saw one youth climb on to the tail plane to get a better view, and before I could stop him he'd gone through it. I managed to get a word in and they quietened down, while Carter, similarly mobbed on the other side, shouted that they were tearing and trampling the Auster to pieces. I pointed out how they were spoiling my aeroplane and that if I didn't get back in it they'd never get liberated. I then produced an impassioned harangue as to how we were coming in great strength as friends and on the following morning would bring them food and put a stop to the bandits; that we were coming (I hoped still) peacefully; and to do as they were told would help more than their numerous offers to point out the collaborators (usually their in-laws, it seemed). I then asked if anyone would risk a trip in the Auster, and a "head man" at that.

'Whereupon about six tried to get into the Auster at once, each with his own gathering of supporters. I picked one with the largest and toughest and noisiest supporters — and partly because he had a magnificent old college crest in gold on a smart blue blazer. I got in too, and got Gunner Carter to wind us up ... I left Gunner Carter as "temporary military governor" and took this smart chap — aged about 30 at a guess — back to the Corps Commander.'

His passenger, a graduate of Rangoon

Akyab, January 1945

The three who spoilt the lovely bombardment
192
Brig John Daniell.
Brig A. J. Daniell
193
Capt Jimmy Jarrett.
Capt C. J. S. Jarrett
194
Gnr Derk Carter.
Capt C. J. S. Jarrett
195
And a quiet landing. *IWM*

University, remained overnight, after which it was announced that the fire support was to be only 'on call'. Jimmy flew back his passenger to the island while other pilots passed the 'cancellation-message' to a suspicious Navy and stood-by ready to observe.

'General Christison himself (XV Corps Commander) was flown over shortly after in an L5,' concludes Jarrett, 'and so took over the military governorship from Gunner Carter'.

After the occupation of Akyab, operations on the west coast of Burma were aimed at pinning the Japanese forces there to prevent their commitment on the Central front. While 82nd West African Division moved south through the hills, a succession of seaborne or river-borne landings were made by 25th Division, with thrusts

therefrom on to the north-to-south tracks. The most determined resistance was met at Kangaw where a fierce battle was fought from 21 January to 17 February, over country where tidal *chaungs* flooded wide areas and made gun positions hard to find, and where the foothills of the Arakan Yomas gave the enemy fields of observation unusual for Burma and very useful to their active artillery.

Ingenuity had to be used to overcome these difficulties, guns being transported up the *chaungs* in lighters, landed by night in mangrove swamps and persuaded by tractor, winch and manpower to selected patches of hard ground. E Troop of 37th Battery of 27th Field Regiment was, in fact, ensconced complete with its four 25pdrs in the lighter *Enterprise*, and engaged the enemy from the vessel's deck, moored in a series of positions around the *chaungs*, both with OPs ashore and with air OP observation.

Before the Kangaw battle was over, another had started twenty-five miles to the south, in preparation for landings north and south of Ru-ywa. *Enterprise's* sister ship *Fighter* now appeared, as 'troop-position' for F Troop of 37th Battery, the CRA hoisted his pennant in HMIS *Narbada* and few resemblances to a land battle seemed to remain. For the actual landings, however, a neighbouring island ('Gun Island', of course) was appropriated and 27th Field Regiment, with a 5.5in troop of 6th Medium Regiment, was landed by night, dug-in and was in action by daybreak. Ru-ywa was captured, 26th Division occupied Ramree Island and 52nd West African Division advanced another 170 miles down the coast by 13 May.

Slim's plan for the dissolution of the Japanese position in Central Burma was bold and inspired. XXXIII Corps was to take over responsibility for clearing the zone between the rivers

Around the chaungs beyond Akyab

196
Lt D. A. Imlay and Gnr Kelly of 8 Field Regiment on their way to an OP near Kangaw. *IWM*
197
Z Craft *Enterprise*, 37/47 Battery of 27 Field Regiment, February 1945. *IWM*

Burma — the decisive battle, February-March 1945.

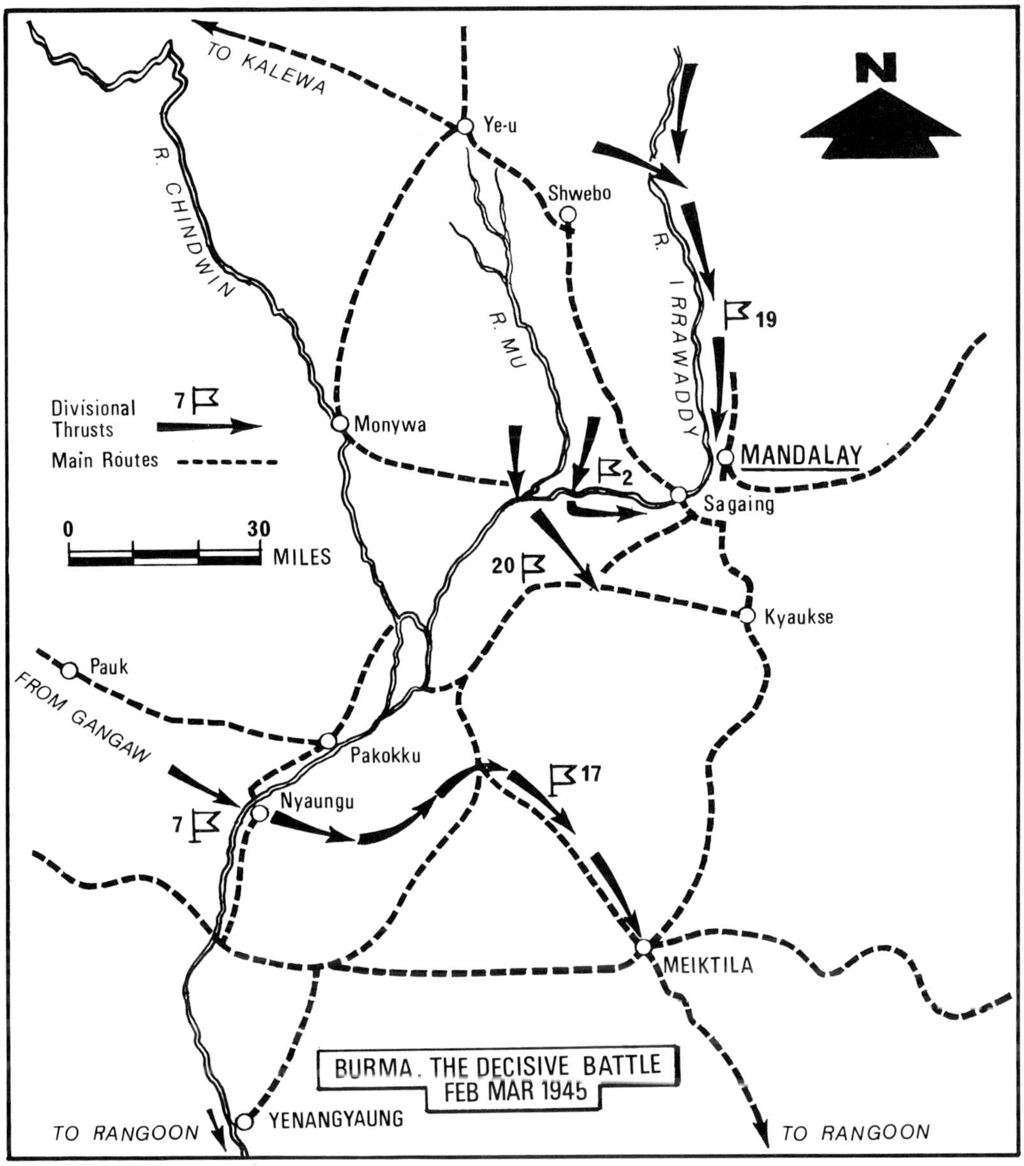

Chindwin and Irrawaddy, after which crossings of the latter were to be made by 19th Indian Division north of Mandalay and by 20th Indian Division west of that city, 2nd British Division closing up to the river between 20th Division and Mandalay itself. With Japanese attention drawn towards Mandalay and its surroundings, IV Corps, disguised as a much smaller body, was to move down the Gangaw valley, cross the Irrawaddy near Nyaungu and make straight across the Burmese plain to seize the communication centre and airfields of Meiktila.

19th Division crossed the Irrawaddy from west to east on 14 and 15 January 1945, at two points 50 and 70 miles north of Mandalay and moved down the east bank towards that city. On 12 February 20th Division started to cross 35 miles west of Mandalay.

114th Field Regiment was still in that division and Sgt Ralph Billings recalls the crossing.

'The Engineers conjured out of nothing a "flotilla" with which to cross this mighty river. Every night at dusk the Corps artillery, 120 guns, threw a tremendous barrage across at the opposite bank. This was a new experience for us and the mighty roar of 25-prs and 5.5s gave us tremendous encouragement, up to then we had had no front line and had not taken part in co-ordinated artillery fire.

' "D" day duly arrived. Two intrepid Marine Commandos swam across in the night and planted lights to mark the bounds of our landing area. Our little canvas boats, weighed down with 12 to 15 men (I was so heavily loaded I could only get up with assistance) were powered across with small outboard motors. The element of surprise had been achieved and although the Japs became aware that something was on and of course expected us somewhere, sweeping the river with machine gun fire, they could see nothing. For once the dark nights we had so hated previously, praying for the first glimmer of light, were on our side. Despite our fears, being well aware of the frailty of our craft and of the impossibility of swimming weighed down as we were, we made the far bank. Wading in with the water up to our chests, the batteries of our wireless sets were ruined and all our early orders to our guns had to be passed through the infantry lightweight sets which they had been able to hold head high on landing. We clambered up the shallow bank and took cover for the night in a deserted village where all night the infantry were subjected to what we called "jitter attacks". Morning light gave me my first sight of Jap fanaticism; an officer was hanging on the wire — too wounded to free himself, he had blown himself up with his own grenade rather than face the inevitable capture.'

The Japanese fiercely attacked this small Irrawaddy bridgehead; the guns engaged them, from the north bank at first and then, crossing on large locally-constructed rafts, from positions in soft sand on the southern side. Battery Sgt-Maj Frank Burbidge recalls these latter gun positions:
'Our position was on the very edge of the water with everything, in direct contradiction of the training manuals, being dug-in in front of the guns. The GPO was calling his orders, the cooks were getting the meals, all literally looking down the barrels of the guns. We were cheek by jowl with the other Field Regiment in the Division, the 9th Field, a regular regiment, so close in fact that one night the 9th opened-up on their SOS lines having heard the signal come into our gun position.'

In the breakout from the bridgehead the OPs were necessarily in the thick of the fighting. Capt Fred Maller, FOO of 232 Battery and supporting an infantry company, 'stood up in full view of the enemy' (in the words of his second medal-citation within a fortnight) 'and urged forward not only his own party but also the leading rifle platoon'. In his unit's War Diary he was described as having 'pursued enemy south'.
One day after the start of 20th Div-

ision's crossing, and 70 miles to the south-west, IV Corps seized a bridgehead with 7th Indian Division and on 21 February passed through 17th Division for Meiktila. Its spearhead was 255th Indian Tank Brigade Group, including 59th Battery of 18th Field Regiment. This battery was equipped with self-propelled 105mm Priests — rare birds indeed in the Burma theatre. With one stiff action on the way, this brigade group captured the first of the Meiktila airfields on 24 February, whereupon a further brigade was flown in. The town of Meiktila was encircled and Japanese reaction became more violent. On 3 March a strong force was dislodged from the Mandalay road, with the capture of several guns, by a squadron of tanks, two companies of infantry and the support of 59th Battery; on the following day the town of Meiktila was occupied.

2nd Division crossed the Irrawaddy on 24 February; their artillery had already been heavily engaged in support of 20th Division's crossing. Soon after the crossing, men of 99th Field Regiment discovered a telephone cable, tapped it and, with the aid of Japanese-speaking liaison staff, interpreted what they heard. Lt-Col R. L. T. Burges, writing in the *RA Commemoration Book*, describes the sequel.
'They heard a Jap RTO (Railway Traffic Officer) in a village a mile or two ahead detailing his departure programme for that night and describing a train loaded in the station. 394th Battery shot-up the station and was disappointed to hear the RTO announce that the rounds were falling near a pagoda 200 yards away. The pagoda was marked on the map and the battery commander corrected his fire. The train was found burning next morning.'

'Perhaps', commented Burges, 'the only occasion in which a Jap, and an RTO at that, ranged a British battery'.
19th Division, meanwhile, had advanced on Mandalay from the northeast of the Irrawaddy — and on 11 March captured Mandalay Hill. A long struggle then took place for the city and finally for Fort Dufferin. Repeated efforts by bombing and rocket attacks having failed, 6in howitzers of 134th Medium Regiment, and also 5.5in guns of 5/22nd Battery attached from 1st Medium Regiment,

199
The road to Meiktila, February 1945; 105mm Priests of 59 Field Battery. *IWM*

were brought into action to bombard the walls at ranges of 300 to 500 yards. On the afternoon of 20 March six Burmese, with white flag and Union Jack, emerged from the east gate and informed the Gunners that the Japanese had gone. Troops of 62nd Brigade entered the Fort and, to quote the *Official History of the War against Japan* (HMSO): 'At 1.30 pm a gunner of the Medium Regiment, a detachment of which went in with the infantry, nailed a Union Jack to the fort flagstaff. Kipling himself, who immortalised Mandalay, could not have thought of a more suitable ending to the battle.'

After the crossings of the Irrawaddy and the battles of Meiktila and Mandalay, the Japanese continued to fight tenaciously. Artillery support was always needed and was often provided

Mandalay, March 1945

200
5.5in gun of 1 Medium Regiment (but attached 134 Medium Regiment) bombarding the walls of Fort Dufferin. *IWM*

201
Maj-Gen T. W. Rees, GOC 19 Division, with his CRA Brig J. A. Macdonald (left) and gunners of 134 Regiment, after the fall of Fort Dufferin. *IWM*

with the power and flexibility conferred by the gunnery developments of the last few years. The climax had passed, however. IV Corps pushed rapidly down the railway valley from Meiktila to Pegu, while XXXIII Corps moved down the Irrawaddy. On 1 May 50th Indian Parachute Brigade was dropped south of Rangoon and on the next day 26th Indian Division made a seaborne landing. Rangoon, however, had already been evacuated by all but small parties of Japanese and, apart from considerable forces trapped in the hills between the railway valley and the west coast, the Japanese armies were now on the line of the River Sittang, 100 miles north-east of Rangoon.

On 6 and 9 August 1945 the Atomic Bombs fell on Hiroshima and Nagasaki, on the 14th Japan accepted unconditional surrender, and very soon veterans of the Burma war were confronted with the incredible sight of Japanese soldiers handing-in their arms.

The war was over.

Conclusion

And so ends this record, of a kind, of the Royal Regiment of Artillery, and sometimes of the artilleries of India and Malta, not a history but rather a

small piece of mosaic from which the imaginative reader might deduce the whole.

The story is of regiments, batteries and smaller detachments of artillery of many varieties, in widely separated theatres of war, climates and operational situations. These batteries were composed of soldiers, prewar regulars and territorials, volunteers and conscripts from civilian life, never

202
On the Sittang River, August 1945. 4.2in mortars of 33 Anti-tank Regiment. *IWM*

203
'The incredible sight' of Japanese soldiers handing in their arms. *IWM*

forgetting the girls of the ATS. It was these soldiers — gun detachments, drivers, wireless-operators, tele-phonists and linesmen, observation post and command post personnel, radar and predictor detachments, in ranks from gunner to major — who gave life to the batteries and whose skill, strength, endurance, precision, courage, command and (above all) team-work enabled the batteries to serve the units and formations they supported. When battles were lost the artillery was sometimes blamed; in victory the infantry and armour were always quick to proclaim the Gunners' part in it.

800,000 served, in the Royal Artillery alone, during World War 2, and of these 28,924 died. These numbers are too large for analysis or for the isolation of prodigies and heroes. Those mentioned in these pages — Lt Pinnington and Sgt Gould at Beda Fomm, RSM Clarke and BSM Batten at Tobruk, Sgt Barbara by the Grand Harbour of Valetta, Brig Campbell and 2-Lt Ward Gunn at Sidi Rezegh, Lt-Col Seely in the Cauldron, Bombardier Johnson laying his gun one-armed at Ruweisat, Sgt Henderson at Sidi Nsir, Havildar Umrao Singh near Tinma, Capt Porteous at Dieppe, Gnr Martin the determined escaper of 1940, and many others — must be regarded as but representative of the whole.

In higher ranks and appointments eighteen Gunner officers commanded Divisions, six Corps or equivalent for-mations, and Gen Sir Alan Cunningham an Army in the field. Two field-marshals, Lords Ironside and Alan-brooke, filled the highest and most responsible British Army appointment (that of CIGS) for all but seventeen months of the war. Generals Sir Ronald Adam and Sir Wilfrid Lindsell played leading parts in administrative fields.

In the peace which has shakily followed World War 2, the Gunners' part on the battlefield, as ever, has tended to be forgotten or undervalued. The present-day infantryman, for example, has never had the formidable experience of observing an enemy attack forming-up for the kill, of recog-nising himself as part of their quarry, of calling for artillery support, of four minutes of suspense and then the crash of shell from 70 guns, scenes of carnage and chaos and the enemy's confused recoil.

With such a picture as background, we can recognise the development of British artillery fire-power from small and primitive beginnings in 1939 to the dominant scale, speed and accuracy of the final years of the war. The advance of anti-aircraft effectiveness was, as we have seen, due to a number of factors, but with the foresight and touch of Gen Sir Frederick Pile very noticeable throughout. For the field-artillery revolution — it was nothing short of a revolution — history should give due prominence to another very modest man but inspired artilleryman. It was, as we have seen, the clear brain of Lt-Col Jack Parham who saw, as early as 1940, what was required and how it could be achieved, and it was Brig Parham who translated his proposal into practical and successful demonstration. By good fortune he then held in turn the key artillery appointments of BRA First Army in North Africa and BRA Second Army in North-west Europe, and so was able to ensure the continued application of his principles. It is not surprising that Field-Marshal Sir Bernard Montgomery, soon after the end of the fighting in Germany, paid the tribute to the Gunners which appears on the facing-page, referring not only to the Gunners who fought with him in his last campaign but to the performance of the artillery as a whole and the standards attained by it in the Second World War.

The words of this tribute serve very well to honour the British and associated artillerymen, from gunner to field-marshal, as they waited and were ready, toiled, fought, suffered and triumphed, in every theatre of war — UBIQUE.

205

205
Service of Dedication of the addition to the Royal Artillery War Memorial to commemorate Gunners who died in World War 2, unveiled by HRH Princess Elizabeth 29 May 1949.
Keystone Press Agency Ltd

206
Royal Artillery Charitable Fund

I would like to pay a compliment to
the gunners, and I would like this to be
passed on to every gunner.

The gunners have risen to great heights in
this war; they have been well commanded
and well handled. In my experience the
artillery has never been so efficient as it
is today; it is at the top of its form.
For all this I offer you my warmest
congratulations.

The contribution of the artillery to final
victory in the German war has been
immense. This will always be so; the
harder the fighting and the longer the
war, the more the infantry, and in
fact all the arms, lean on the gunners.
The proper use of the artillery is a great
battle-winning factor.

I think all the other arms have done very
well too. But the artillery has been
terrific and I want to give due weight
to its contribution to the victory in this
campaign.

B. L. Montgomery
Field-Marshal
C-in-C
21 Army Group.

Germany
27-6-45

Bibliography

Books

Official (Cabinet Office); *History of the Second World War*; All Theatres, Various Volumes; HMSO.

Bidwell, Shelford; *Gunners at War*; Arms & Armour

Blaxland, Gregory; *The Plain Cook and the Great Showman*; William Kimber

Churchill, Winston S.; *The Second World War, Vols I to VI*; Cassell

Collier, Basil; *The Battle of the V-Weapons, 1944-45*; Hodder & Stoughton

Duncan, Brig W. E. & others, Eds; *The Royal Artillery Commemoration Book, 1939-1945*; RA Benevolent Fund

Hogg, Ian V.; *British and American Artillery of Word War 2*; Arms & Armour

Longhurst, Henry; *I wouldn't have Missed it*; J. M. Dent & Sons

MacFetridge, C. H. T. and Warren, J. P.; *Tales of the Mountain Gunners*; William Blackwood

Milligan, Spike; *Rommel? Gunner Who?,* and *Mussolini, His Part in my Downfall*; Michael Joseph

Ministry of Information; *Roof over Britain*; HMSO

Parham, Maj-Gen H. J., and Belfield, E. M. G.; *Unarmed into Battle*; Warren & Son

Phillips, C. E. Lucas; *Springboard to Victory*; Heinemann

Pile, Gen Sir Frederick; *Ack-Ack*; George G. Harrap

Shulman, Milton; *Defeat in the West*; Secker & Warburg

Periodicals

Gunner, various numbers.

Journal of Army Aviation, 1973

Journal of the Royal Artillery, various numbers.